602017

W9-ATE-031

More Advance Praise

"Authored by two of the most insightful Southern intellectuals of our time, *The Southernization of America* is well worth a read by anyone trying to understand American politics in the aftermath of Trump."
— **Adam H. Domby, author of** *The False Cause: Fraud, Fabrication, and White Supremacy in Confederate Memory*

"Necessary reading for all who would understand the current crisis in which the nation finds itself—turned against its ideals and turned toward abiding bigotry. Knowing how we got here is a critical step toward finding a way out."— **Alice Randall, author of** *Black Bottom Saints*

"Tucker and Gaillard explore the lingering influence of the old Confederacy on modern American politics. One reads this book with a shock of recognition and dismay, but also with the hope that the leaders of the future may emerge from the battlegrounds of the past."
— **Lawrence Wright, Pulitzer-winning author of** *The Plague Year* **and** *The Looming Tower*

"Indispensable reading on how the promise of American democracy remains under siege by violence and hate—and what will be required to ensure it has a fighting chance." — **Sarah Posner, author of** *Unholy: How White Christian Nationalists Powered the Trump Presidency, and the Devastating Legacy They Left Behind*

"Tucker and Gaillard have deconstructed how their beloved South, always desperate to find an exportable commodity, continues to discover ready markets for the xenophobia, white supremacy, and hypocrisy that defined it for decades. And yet the authors connect dots that give Americans of goodwill hope for the future."
— **Hank Klibanoff, coauthor of** *The Race Beat: The Press, the Civil Rights Struggle and the Awakening of a Nation*, **and creator of the Peabody Award-winning podcast,** *Buried Truths*

"A smart, transformative book. Helps explain why the best and the worst of American politics today ties back to the history of the South." — **Ben Montgomery, author of** *A Shot in the Moonlight*

"With a journalistic eye for detail, Gaillard and Tucker present a bracing account of America's reckoning with race and justice over the past half-century. The result is a sobering but clarifying narrative of where we've been, and a call to persevere in pursuit of our democratic ideals." — **Kristin Kobes Du Mez, author of** *Jesus and John Wayne: How White Evangelicals Corrupted a Faith and Fractured a Nation*

"Building on John Egerton's foundation of studying the South within a national framework, Gaillard and Tucker show that any tour of recent American political life goes through the South. The book urges us to ask if we should consider Donald Trump a Southern president." — **Ted Ownby, William F. Winter Professor of History and Southern Studies, University of Mississippi**

"Tucker and Gaillard sketch a picture of a modern America shaped by multiracial freedom struggles as well as by the vicious, protean structures of white supremacy. *The Southernization of America* issues a charge to its readers: choose democracy in defiance of our country's most narrow impulses and with a resolve equal to that of previous generations, or else." — **Adriane Lentz-Smith, author of** *Freedom Struggles: African Americans and World War I*

THE
SOUTHERNIZATION
OF AMERICA

The Southernization of America

A Story of
Democracy in the Balance

FRYE GAILLARD
AND CYNTHIA TUCKER

NewSouth Books
Montgomery

To Mary L. Marshall Tucker,
and in loving memory of John A. Tucker

NewSouth Books
105 S. Court Street
Montgomery, AL 36104

Publisher's Cataloging-in-Publication Data
Names: Gaillard, Frye, 1946– , and Tucker, Cynthia, 1955– ,authors.
Title: The southernization of America : a story of democracy in the balance / Frye
Gaillard and Cynthia Tucker.
Description: Montgomery, AL : NewSouth Books, [2022] | Includes index. |
Identifiers: LCCN 2021045565 (print) | ISBN 9781588384560 (hardback) | ISBN
978158838460 (ebook)
Subjects: Politics and government—United States—the South—19th–21st centuries
| Race relations—United States—the South—19th–21st centuries | Civil rights—
History—20th century | Social Culture—United States—20th–21st centuries |
Voting rights—United States—the South—19th–21st centuries.

Design by Randall Williams

Printed in the United States of America by Sheridan

*The Black Belt, defined by its dark, rich soil, stretches across central
Alabama. It was the heart of the cotton belt. It was and is a place of
great beauty, of extreme wealth and grinding poverty, of pain and joy.
Here we take our stand, listening to the past, looking to the future.*

Contents

Note to Readers

This book was suggested to coauthors Cynthia Tucker and Frye Gaillard by NewSouth's editor, Randall Williams. All three were friends of and are admirers of John Egerton and know well his work of four decades ago, *The Americanization of Dixie*, now rendered sadly ironic. The present volume represents the combined reflections of Tucker and Gaillard, veteran journalists who are now colleagues at the University of South Alabama. Both are Alabama natives with family roots running deep in the South. Tucker is African American, Gaillard is white. Over their careers, both have written extensively about their home region. Of the alternating essays that follow, those with first-person references carry the byline of the primary author. Each chapter explores the undeniable Southern influence—for better or worse—on the life and political climate of America.

THE
SOUTHERNIZATION
OF AMERICA

Introduction

In 1974, the great Southern journalist John Egerton wrote a prescient book entitled *The Americanization of Dixie: The Southernization of America*. In a series of connected but self-contained essays, he made the point that something fundamental was changing—both in his native South, and in the country as a whole. But even Egerton seemed not to be sure exactly how things would unfold.

He was, as those of us who knew him could attest, one of the great and gentle souls of his time, a man deeply committed to racial justice who wanted badly to believe that it would be a good thing if this troubled place in which he lived—this part of America that had once fought a war for the right to own slaves—could emerge from the strife of the civil rights years somehow chastened and wiser for the journey; if it could narrow its distance from the rest of the country and perhaps even lead it toward better days. That was the hope. But Egerton, as was his habit, saw darker possibilities as well. Giving voice to his fears, he wrote:

> The South and the nation are not exchanging strengths as much as they are exchanging sins; more often than not, they are sharing and spreading the worst in each other, while the best languishes and withers. There are exceptions, of course . . . But the dominant trends are unmistakable: deep divisions along race and class lines, an obsession with growth and acquisition

and consumption, a headlong rush to the cities and suburbs, diminution and waste of natural resources, institutional malfunctioning, abuse of political and economic power, increasing depersonalization, and a steady erosion of a sense of place, of community, of belonging.

FOR A WHILE IT was easy enough to make the case that Egerton's gloom was misplaced, or at least overstated. The anecdotal evidence was all around. In Virginia, Republican governor Linwood Holton had stunned political observers when he was elected in 1969 on a promise of racial reconciliation. In contrast to the Southern Democrats who had controlled Virginia for a hundred years, Holton proclaimed that the "era of defiance"—of resistance to civil rights progress—was coming to an end. He supported school desegregation, appointed women and minorities to state government, and promised to make Virginia "a model in race relations." In Florida, new Democratic governor Reubin Askew sounded nearly identical themes. He supported busing as a tool for integrating schools—a moral and educational imperative, he said—and while appointing African Americans to the highest levels of state government, he set such a standard for integrity and competence that Harvard's John F. Kennedy School of Government rated him one of the top ten governors of the twentieth century. And, of course, there was Jimmy Carter. Elected governor of Georgia in 1970, Carter proclaimed in his inaugural address that "the time for racial discrimination is over." Easily the most ambitious of these New South champions, he soon set out for the presidency with Southernness at the heart of his appeal. He said:

I've been the product of an emerging South. I see the clear advantages of throwing off the millstone of racial prejudice. I think it's a process that's compatible with the moral and ethical standards of our nation—the heritage of our country, as envisioned by our forefathers. I also see that we have a special responsibility here. When we are meek, or quiescent, or silent on the subject of civil rights at home or human rights abroad, there is no other voice on Earth that can replace the lost voice, the absent voice, of the United States. This is what the persecutors want, and this is what the persecuted fear.

For many Americans, it was mesmerizing—a peanut farmer from the deepest South reconnecting the country with its finest ideals. In 1976, when Carter won the Democratic nomination, he stood side by side at the national convention, gazing out across the sea of delegates, with Martin Luther King Sr. There they were, two native Georgians, one black, one white, a Southern governor and a civil rights lion, sharing a moment that felt like a revival—not only of the faith they both proclaimed, but of a dream deferred—of shining hopes and possibilities in which so many of us wanted to believe.

"Surely the Lord," shouted Daddy King over the mad cacophony of music and cheers amid descending balloons, "is in this place."

THERE WAS INTOXICATION IN the moment, but we knew it was shadowed by something very different—the realities John Egerton was writing about. In the presidential election of 1968, Richard Nixon had embarked on a Southern strategy, and he did not mean the things that Jimmy Carter was telling us. In a sense, Nixon's mentor had been George Wallace. He watched in private admiration as the Alabama governor, who had pledged in 1963 his commitment to "segregation forever," learned to redefine his appeal. In the presidential primaries of 1964 and '68, Wallace spoke more obliquely about race, almost as if he were teaching the nation how to think in code.

From the time he famously stood in the schoolhouse door, he had begun to polish that skill. Everybody understood in the summer of 1963 the mission at hand, how Wallace was embarked on a doomed, quixotic quest to block the admission of black students Vivian Malone and James Hood to the University of Alabama. But just as secessionists a hundred years earlier had talked about states' rights when they really meant slavery, Wallace cast the federal government as a bully—an outside force pursuing integration without regard for the will of the people—and himself as a noble defender of freedom. A few years later, on the campaign trail for the presidency, he found it useful not to mention segregation but to talk about "liberal sob sisters," or "bleeding heart sociologists," or "some bearded Washington bureaucrat who can't even park a bicycle straight."

All the shared resentments were there, but he and his audience felt shielded from the charge—his accusers frustrated as they attempted to make it—that they were bigots at heart. There were times when he couldn't contain himself. Once in 1968 he invoked the specter of urban riots—those moments when African American rage, often in response to police brutality, erupted into violence; became, in a sense, a magnified reflection of the crime.

"We don't have riots down in Alabama," Wallace roared,

bantam-weight defiance flashing in his eyes. "They start a riot down there, first one of 'em to pick up a brick gets a bullet to the brain. And then you walk over to the next one and say, 'All right, pick up a brick. We just want to see you pick up one of them bricks, now!' "

Newsman Douglas Kiker of NBC, observing the response of a Midwestern crowd, was struck by a sudden, horrifying epiphany: "They all hate black people, all of them. They're all afraid . . . Great God! That's it! They're all Southern! The whole United States is Southern!"

There were African American activists, people like James Baldwin or Malcolm X, who begged to differ. Both had written with urgency about the indigenous racism of the North. But if the story was more complicated, if racism had already taken root in every nook and corner of America, was there nevertheless something in Kiker's moment of revelation? In this era of homogenization, when television and interstate highways—and soon enough, the internet—were erasing the isolation of the South, pulling it into the national mainstream, was there something about our place that was beginning to reshape the country? And if there was, might it be a source of mystical promise? Or was it, more inevitably, a reality overflowing with dread?

In the following essays, more reflections than a narrative history, we consider the Southernization of America from the time John Egerton coined the term—the eve of the Carter presidency—through the toxic era of Donald Trump. It may well be (as some have also said of Black History) that the story of the South *is* the story of America . . . with all the implied pain and promise.

The Fragile Promise

Frye Gaillard and Cynthia Tucker

In the beginning, the thing that set him apart was ambition. Jimmy Carter had been governor for less than two years when he attended the Democratic National Convention and toyed half seriously with the possibility of becoming George McGovern's running mate. Certainly, there were those in his entourage, including young aide Hamilton Jordan, who were quick to push his case.

McGovern, however, was not very interested, and for Carter it was probably just as well. McGovern in 1972 represented the liberal wing of the Democratic Party. He was a war hero who hated war—a B-24 pilot during World War II, who flew thirty-five missions behind German lines and won the Distinguished Flying Cross. As a U.S. Senator from South Dakota, he opposed the War in Vietnam—all the devastation of our napalm and bombs, and progress measured in body counts, and the division the war was causing at home. He lost overwhelmingly to Richard Nixon, and Jimmy Carter, who kept his distance, was spared the taint of the Democratic disaster.

In September 1972, two months before the Nixon landslide, Hamilton Jordan and Gerald Rafshoon, another of Carter's young aides, went to him with an improbable aspiration. "Governor," they said, "we'd like to have a talk about your future." They urged him to make his own run for the presidency, and it was a measure of Carter's burning ambition that he told them he was thinking about it. Then he smiled and added: "Don't tell anybody. It sounds too ridiculous."

It began to sound less so as the Vietnam war raged on and Nixon's presidency dissolved into scandal. When Nixon resigned amid the shame of Watergate—a corruption that would prove to be a warm-up for the new millennium—Carter began to campaign full-time for a goal that suddenly seemed within reach. He was a man with an engineer's mind, a quality nurtured at the U.S. Naval Academy. With technocratic precision, he later explained, "we memorized all the state election laws" and set off on a fifty-state quest to meet with grass-roots Democrats. In living rooms and small convention halls, he subjected himself to the curiosity and skepticism of Democratic leaders, many startled by the force of his intelligence.

"At those kinds of sessions, Jimmy Carter was a genius," remembered James Fallows, long-time correspondent for the *Atlantic*, who once served as a Carter speechwriter. "There is, I think, an important contrast between his impressiveness in small groups and his larger difficulties as a political leader. But in 1976, some pretty hard-nosed Democratic leaders . . . came away thinking Jimmy Carter was FDR."

Part of their fascination inevitably lay in the fact that Carter was Southern. Here was a politician whose decency had been steeled by the most important issue of his time, who could project the experience of the civil rights years into a sense of mission for America. But others were not so sure. Robert Sam Anson, who wrote a cover story about Carter for *New Times* magazine, was one of literally hundreds of journalists who flocked to the South to try to understand this enigmatic governor with a Georgia accent and oversized smile, who was not what they had in mind for a president. Anson wrote:

> The South, more than anything, I guess, it was what had secretly bothered me about Carter—that he was one of them, from there . . . that place. It was not the sort of worry you talked about openly, not unless you were among friends, secure in a Manhattan apartment or in a Georgetown drawing room. And when you owned up to it—admitted that when you heard someone talking with that accent, you mentally clicked down a couple of stops, knowing that whoever he was and whatever he said he did, he thought differently (meaning not as well) than you, lived differently, had different values . . . There was something about those people. They were not Americans in the same way that we were Americans. That place was, in fact, a different country.

THAT SKEPTICISM, BORDERING ON antipathy, with a prosperous Georgia farmer moving inexorably toward the White House, soon propelled Anson on a journey to "that place" so filled with mystery and revelation. By the time Anson left the South, having traveled its back roads and interstate highways for a month, he amazed himself by writing these words: "If there were any hope left for this country, any hope at all, it was here . . . in Dixie."

Among the stops Anson made was one in Charlotte, North Carolina. He found a proud city emerging from a crisis, for Charlotte in the early 1970s had been the national test case for busing. In 1971, the U.S. Supreme Court upheld an order by U.S. District Judge James B. McMillan, a native Southerner, requiring busing, if that's what it took, to completely desegregate the schools. The response of the community was immediate and bitter. Mobs of white protesters regularly besieged the school system's headquarters. At one time or another during the first several years, racial fighting closed every high school in the system. McMillan was hanged in effigy, and the offices of Julius Chambers, the African American lawyer in the case, were burned to the ground.

By 1976, however, Charlotte had come to a different place. Under a new busing plan designed by a grass-roots citizens committee and approved by McMillan, peace had been restored. Test scores in the schools were rising, white flight was minor, and everywhere Anson went, people seemed proud of what they had accomplished. "Busing has worked in Charlotte," he wrote with some astonishment, for the story was such a contrast to cities like Boston—cities in the North—where the outcome had been much different.

No one intrigued Anson more than McMillan, who seemed to be a man who was Southern to the bone: bespectacled, soft-spoken, a Harvard-trained lawyer, raised in the swampy flatlands of eastern North Carolina, whose delicate job during World War II had been defusing bombs. He possessed a kind of fatalistic grace as he deflected questions on the effigy hangings and threats on his life, or the subtler ostracism by his former friends at the Charlotte Country Club. "But there was too much pain in the gray eyes," Anson wrote, "to hide the torment he had gone through, even if he politely refused to talk about it."

McMillan, in a sense, embodied both the bravery and the cost of a community coming to terms with its past.

Anson would visit other Southern cities—Atlanta, Nashville, Charleston—but he was drawn also to the rural places, about which the great James Baldwin had written with dread. In an article for *Harper's* in 1958, Baldwin described his first glimpse of the Southern landscape, the rust-red soil he could see through the window as his airplane descended toward Atlanta. He said he could not suppress the thought

> that this earth had acquired its color from the blood that had dripped down from these trees. My mind was filled with the image of a black man, younger than I, perhaps, or my own age, hanging from a tree, while white men watched him and cut out his sex with a knife . . . The Southern landscape—the trees, the silence, the liquid heat, and the fact that one always seems to be traveling great distances—seems designed for violence, seems, almost, to demand it. What passions cannot be unleashed on a Southern night!

As ANSON BEGAN HIS uneasy trek through the Southern outback, he traveled for a time with Ray Jenkins, editorial page editor of the *Alabama Journal* in Montgomery. Jenkins, who would soon become a spokesman for Jimmy Carter's State Department, was wise in the ways of the South. One of the stops he made with Anson was the village of Hayneville, where they went to see John Hulett, the first black sheriff of Lowndes County, Alabama. Lowndes was nestled between Selma and Montgomery, and much of the iconic march of 1965 had followed U.S. Highway

80 past cotton fields and rolling pastureland and dips through moss-draped swamps—the haunted, blood-soaked landscape of Lowndes. Two infamous murders had occurred in the county in 1965. Viola Liuzzo, a white woman from Michigan who came for the Selma to Montgomery march, was gunned down hours after it ended. Five months later, after Congress had passed the Voting Rights Act, Jonathan Daniels, a white Episcopal seminarian who supported civil rights, was shotgunned to death at point-blank range by a prominent local white man named Thomas Coleman.

In the immediate aftermath of those murders, John Hulett was part of a cadre of activists who founded what became the Black Panther Party. Its official name was the Lowndes County Freedom Organization, a political party with a panther as its ballot symbol, formed to register black voters and support the wave of African Americans newly emboldened to run for political office. One of the volunteers who came to Lowndes County to support this effort was Huey Newton, a young Californian who admired the militancy of people like Hulett. Newton carried their symbol back to Oakland and in 1966 helped form the Black Panther Party for Self-Defense. Hulett was never sure what to make of Newton, who seemed to be spoiling for a fight. Hulett was not like that. By the time of Robert Sam Anson's visit, some of us had come to regard Hulett as a kind of Nelson Mandela of the Black Belt.

As sheriff, he worked to be colorblind, and one of his staunch supporters by then was—remarkably—Tom Coleman, the infamous civil rights murderer. Their cautious friendship began in 1970, five years after the Daniels murder, when Hulett announced he was running for sheriff.

"John," asked Coleman, "what are you and your folks going to do?"

"Well, Tom," Hulett replied, "I'm running for sheriff, and I think I'm going to win."

"That's okay," said Coleman. "I'm leaving the county."

Hulett responded with a level gaze. "We didn't leave when you were in charge."

He went on to say that the electoral victories now looming for blacks—this brave new world of biracial democracy—would not usher in an era of revenge, just an era of fair dealing and equality. He wondered if Coleman could handle such a thing.

Some time later, after Hulett had won and assumed the mantle of Lowndes County sheriff, his telephone rang in the middle of the night. It was Coleman, who had been listening, he said, to the police scanner. There had been an accident on I-65—a truck overturned near the town of Fort Deposit, its contents scattered all over the highway. Coleman offered to meet him there and help with the cleanup. Hulett had to wonder. This was a dark and lonesome stretch of road, and it hadn't been long since Coleman had killed and gotten away with it. But the sheriff said fine, come on down, and the two of them worked until almost morning, cleaning up the debris.

That was the way it went until Tom Coleman's death. This middle-aged killer of Jonathan Daniels, this dour and unremarkable man with lines on his face and a look of furtive sadness in his eyes, became one of John Hulett's most dependable supporters. Not everyone saw Coleman that way, of course. To some, he was merely an unrepentant racist who had committed an unspeakable crime. But Hulett thought Coleman was trying to reach out, trying in his gruff and uncertain way to seek forgiveness for this thing he had done. Maybe, said Hulett, this was all the bravery Coleman could muster.

Charles V. Hamilton, a political scientist at Columbia University who as an African American activist had volunteered in the Alabama Black Belt, came to know John Hulett well. He thought he saw the same qualities in Lowndes County that he would later see in South Africa. From Mandela to Hulett, these were people with no hatred in their hearts and no interest in revenge. "None whatsoever," said Hamilton.

NOT LONG AFTER RAY Jenkins returned to Montgomery, having introduced Hulett to Robert Sam Anson, he found himself writing a quite remarkable story of his own. On a Sunday morning in 1979, George Wallace, now confined to a wheelchair, paid a visit to Martin Luther King's former church in Montgomery. Seven years earlier, on a campaign stop in Maryland, Wallace had been shot through the spine by a white man, a mentally disturbed unemployed janitor. Wallace had won five Democratic presidential primaries in 1972, with law and order the heart of his message. But now it was over. Now he lay in a hospital bed, depressed, in pain, paralyzed from the waist down.

His daughter Peggy was keeping vigil when an unexpected visitor came. Congresswoman Shirley Chisholm was also running for president in 1972. More symbolically than Wallace perhaps, she was seeking the Democratic nomination, the first black woman ever to do so. On the campaign trail and as a member of Congress, she was a fierce advocate for the dispossessed, for women and children and people of color—the ideological opposite of Wallace, most people would have said. But now here she was, standing next to his hospital bed, speaking softly, gently, telling him that this terrible thing "should not happen to anybody." Peggy Wallace Kennedy remembered them praying.

She thought her father was never the same after that, thought the visit set him off on a long and painful journey of introspection, sometimes self-serving and defensive, tinged with self-pity, but sometimes more honest than that. And so on a 1979 Sunday at Dexter Avenue King Memorial Baptist Church, aides wheeled Wallace down the aisle to the storied pulpit, and he told the worshippers: "I have learned what suffering means. I think I can understand something of the pain black people have come to endure. I know I have contributed to that pain and I can only ask for forgiveness."

The people believed him, or so it seemed to Ray Jenkins, for as the choir sang and the congregation prayed, many wept and reached out to touch him. There were skeptics, of course. Alabama journalist Bob Ingram said that many people thought Wallace was "merely auditioning for heaven." Others noted that the governor "knew how to count." In these years after the 1965 Voting Rights Act, African Americans had become a political force to be reckoned with.

John Lewis was not one of the cynics. The great civil rights leader, a native Alabamian who soon became a member of Congress, would remember several conversations with Wallace, starting in 1979—private moments in which the governor asked for his forgiveness. "It was almost," said Lewis, "like someone confessing to a priest."

This was the South of Jimmy Carter, the one that he presented to the world. It was still a hard land, riddled with poverty in its rural backwaters and economic inequality in its cities. But there were the multiple stories of change—those ripples of redemption that gave people hope. For Carter, as president, and later in his work with the Carter Center in Atlanta, it was an easy transition from support of civil rights in the South to a defense of basic freedoms everywhere in the world.

Jacobo Timerman, a crusading editor in Argentina, thought Carter and his policies saved thousands of lives, including his own. For thirty months, beginning in 1976, Timerman was one of those jailed and tortured for speaking out against the Argentinian government. He was freed in 1979, largely he said, because of Carter's human rights pressures. Five years later, they met. "We were looking at each other," Timerman remembered. "We are almost the same height, and our faces were at the same level. I said to him, 'How do you feel looking at my face, knowing that you saved my life?' His face flushed red, and he looked down and then he touched my shoulder. We Latins, we are used to embracing. But he is an American, a very shy person, and yet you could see he was moved." Timerman paused for a moment. The year was 1985, and war and dread and the reality of oppression still defined too much of the world. But Carter had offered a respite, he said: "It was the first time—and I fear the last—in this violent and criminal century that a major power has defended human rights all over the world."

But soon it was gone.

IN THE END, JIMMY Carter failed. Whatever his triumphs in the beginning, runaway inflation and a hostage crisis in Iran defined the final months of his presidency, and Americans in 1980 lost confidence in his ability to lead. They turned to a different kind of leader—one who possessed a different vision for the country and not incidentally a very different view of the South. On August 3, early in his presidential campaign, Ronald Reagan made a stop at the Neshoba County Fair in Mississippi. Ten thousand people, nearly all of them white, turned out to see him. Reagan knew the history of this place—how in the summer of 1964, Freedom Summer in Mississippi, three civil rights workers were murdered not far from where he was speaking.

Mickey Schwerner, at twenty-four, was a veteran field organizer for the Congress of Racial Equality (CORE), known to members of the Ku Klux Klan as "the Jew boy with a beard." James Chaney was African American, a native Mississippian who was also already a veteran of the civil rights movement. But Andrew Goodman was different, an anthropology major from Queens College in New York, who volunteered for Freedom Summer, eager, he said, despite the dangers, to help black Mississippians register to vote. He arrived in the state on June 21. Later, his friends would try to imagine his terror when he was arrested that same day with Schwerner and Chaney and jailed in the Neshoba County town of Philadelphia. The three were charged with speeding and released when they paid a twenty-dollar fine.

It was the last time anyone saw them alive.

Two days later, on June 23, Choctaw Indians from a nearby reservation found the burned-out shell of their car. Their bodies were found on August 4, buried within a pond's earthen dam. All three had been shot. The autopsy revealed red clay in Goodman's lungs, a handful also clenched in his fist. Almost certainly, he was buried still alive.

On August 3, 1980, one day short of this grisly anniversary, Reagan spoke about none of these things. Mostly, his talk was genial banter, a politician at the peak of his charm: "People say Jimmy Carter is doing his best—that's our problem." But there was, many people thought, a much darker moment. As the *New York Times* reported on August 4, Reagan told the crowd, "I believe in states' rights." Conservatives insisted that the Republican candidate was simply talking about a theory of government. But as Reagan himself must certainly have known, he had chosen a phrase with a dubious history—one used by secessionists during the Civil War when what they really meant was slavery, or much more recently, the theory of government George Wallace employed when he stood in the schoolhouse door in Alabama. As William Raspberry noted in the *Washington Post*, Reagan was a savvy politician who soon won the heart of Southern Democrats. His campaign speech in Philadelphia, Raspberry wrote, "was an important bouquet in that courtship."

THERE MAY HAVE BEEN more to it. For virtually all of his political career, Reagan was a man unmoved by the sacrifices of the civil rights years, the idealism rippling forth from the place where he spoke about states' rights—all the way west to the state where he decided to run for governor. This happened in 1964, when Mario Savio, a student at Berkeley, returned to California deeply impressed by his own experience during Freedom Summer. Savio spent much of his Mississippi time as a volunteer teacher in a Freedom School, finding young black students eager to learn about things like Black History that never came up in their regular schools. The thing he carried back from Mississippi was less a memory of violence and more an enduring sense of respect for the feeling of community he found in the movement.

"You felt it in the black church, especially," he said. "The singing. You really felt cradled. It's impossible for someone to convey who hasn't experienced it. As much as someone could who, by that time, was very much a secular person, you felt in the bosom of the Lord."

He was amazed to discover when he returned to Berkeley that student activism was forbidden on campus. This included support for a movement he had come to love, one for which he knew people had died. He became the spokesman for a Free Speech Movement, during which he demonstrated an eloquence that some people compared to Martin Luther King's. At one of the demonstrations, he told the six thousand students who assembled—in defiance of university policy—"there's a time when the operation of the machine becomes so odious, makes you so sick at heart, that you can't take part. You can't even passively take part. And you've got to put your bodies upon the gears and upon the wheels, upon the levers, upon all the apparatus, and you've got to make it stop. And you've got to indicate to the people who run it, to the people who own it, that unless you're free the machine will be prevented from working at all."

Joan Baez was there that day, having learned the power of protest music partly through her experience in the South. One of her mentors was Birmingham native Odetta Holmes, who performed simply under the name Odetta. Coming of age in the Great Depression, an African American in the segregated

South, Odetta fell in love with protest songs, which were a way for desperate people to cope. "They were liberation songs," she said. "You're walking down life's road, society's foot is on your throat, every which way you turn you can't get from under that foot. And you reach a fork in the road and you can either lie down and die or insist upon life . . . those people who made up the songs were the ones who insisted upon life."

Baez saw it this way when she added her voice to the civil rights movement or sang "The Times, They Are A'Changin'" for the Free Speech students who gathered at Berkeley. "The more love you can feel," she told the demonstrators, "the more chance there is for it to be a success."

Ronald Reagan was a California actor when all of this was happening, a man beginning to nurse a burning political ambition. He said somebody should "clean up the mess." Two years later, still sounding that theme, he was elected governor of California.

SOME TWENTY YEARS LATER, when he was running for reelection as president, the same imperviousness was on full display. Instead of the Neshoba County Fair, Reagan made a campaign stop in Charlotte. This was where Robert Sam Anson, in his search for the forces that propelled Jimmy Carter, found people who were proud of their integrated schools. But Reagan came with a different message. He criticized Democrats for their support of "busing that takes innocent children out of the neighborhood school and makes them pawns in a social experiment that nobody wants. And we've found out that it failed."

Charlotte school superintendent Jay Robinson, a believer in the benefits of integration, was watching the speech on television.

"That son of a bitch," he snapped, and switched off the set. Robinson was worried, correctly, as it turned out, that the president would give aid and comfort to a nascent anti-busing revival in Charlotte—a movement among people who were new to the city, who came from places where school populations were more homogenous. When it came to matters of race and class, they did not see the value of diversity. They wanted their children in school with students from families just like their own.

On a national level, Reagan was leading in the same direction. In his book, *Overturning Brown: The Segregationist Legacy of the Modern School Choice Movement*, Steve Suitts of Emory University recently wrote that private schools, after Reagan's election, "received federal support and endorsement as never before . . . In his State of the Union Address . . . President Reagan declared: 'We must continue the advance by supporting discipline in our schools, vouchers to give parents freedom of choice; and we must give back to our children their lost right to acknowledge God in their classrooms.'" As Suitts pointed out, these were all too familiar echoes of a time when conservative churches in the South set up academies—almost exclusively white—to resist the march toward desegregation.

"Without attribution," Suitts wrote, "the views and tools of Southern segregationists had become the official position of the national Republican Party and the Reagan presidency."

To many of us, this was the heart of the Reagan legacy.

Some others disagreed—bitterly, if our implication was that Reagan was a racist. Republican strategist Steve Schmidt, who would rail a generation later at the open bigotry of Donald Trump, saw none of that in Reagan. For Schmidt and many others, this fortieth president who came from California remained forever a political hero. There were arguments to support that view. Writing in *National Review*, Deroy Murdock noted that Reagan not only signed an extension of the Voting Rights Act but also the law creating a holiday for Dr. King.

At the latter's signing ceremony, Reagan declared that King "stirred our nation to the very depths of its soul." Coretta Scott King was there that day, and she was moved. "It was a beautiful day," she told the assembled reporters. "And the president spoke as president of all the people today." She did not say whether she thought this was always the case.

Whatever the reality of Reagan's heart, there was no doubt that his charm—the impressiveness of his communication skills—gave a reassuring cover for the uglier side of his party's evolution. In 1980, during primary season for the GOP, young strategist Lee Atwater cast his lot with the Reagan campaign. Atwater was born and raised in South Carolina, and at twenty-nine he was regarded as a wunderkind—effective, ruthless, not at all above dirty tricks, which, in fact, he seemed to enjoy. As the primaries were first taking shape, three candidates were competing for delegates in South Carolina—Reagan, George H. W. Bush, and former Texas governor John Connally, who had once been a Democrat. When a group of African American ministers approached Atwater about working for Reagan, he told them the campaign had no money and suggested they reach out to Connally. When they did, he leaked a story—actually, he arranged for somebody else to do it—that Connally was trying to bribe black ministers in exchange for African American votes. As *Politico* reported years later, "Lee laughed about that story."

NOBODY LAUGHED EIGHT YEARS later when Atwater became a chief strategist for Bush, who was running to succeed Reagan as president. Early in the campaign, Bush's Democratic opponent, Governor Michael Dukakis of Massachusetts, was leading by seventeen points in the polls. Atwater figured that would change. He said he would "strip the bark off the little bastard." He soon saw his chance with the case of Willie Horton, a convicted murderer serving life without parole in Massachusetts, who failed to return from a weekend furlough and raped a white woman in Maryland. He also pistol-whipped her boyfriend.

"By the time we're finished," Atwater promised, "they're going to wonder whether Willie Horton is Dukakis's running mate." Bush talked about the issue on the campaign trail, but it was a television ad, produced conveniently by a conservative PAC not officially connected to the campaign, that touched the marrow of American fear. There on the nation's television sets was a shadowy photograph of Horton, scowling, bearded, projecting a kind of arrogant menace that could chill a white American to the bone. Even without the words of the announcer, you could imagine the kind of things he would do—the things that he had *already* done; things that *any of them* might do—abetted by politicians weak on crime. That was the theory and effect of the ad—not the kernel of truth in the issue, the wisdom of a furlough program available to violent offenders in prison, but broader racial fears in the country, so easily conflated with the issue of crime.

The immediate effect of the ad was immense. Dukakis could see that he was "getting killed." And as other commentators have noted, the next generation of Democratic politicians felt it necessary to cover their flank, to demonstrate to doubting voters that they, too, could be tough on crime.

In 1991, three years after Bush won the presidency, Atwater was sorry for what he had done. In so many ways, he had sailed through life—handsome, talented, successful, smart—but now in the shadow of his fortieth birthday, he was dying with cancer. He wrote in an article for *Life* magazine:

> In 1988, fighting Dukakis, I said that I "would strip the bark off the little bastard" and "make Willie Horton his running mate." I am sorry for both statements: the first for its naked cruelty, the second because it makes me sound like a racist, which I am not.
>
> I acquired more wealth, power and prestige than most. But you can acquire all you want and still feel empty. . . . It took a deadly illness to put me eye to eye with that truth, but it is a truth that the country, caught up in its ruthless ambitions and moral decay, can learn on my dime.

People disagree about deathbed confessions. Do they matter? Did Atwater mean it? Maybe they do, and maybe he did. There is really no reason to think he didn't. But one thing is indisputable: The Republican Party learned nothing on his dime. The next man up among its strategists was Karl Rove, a political consultant who was happy to tear a once grand party from its last and tattered moorings in the truth. In 1994, a decade before his "swift boat" smears against the war record of Democrat John Kerry, Rove was polishing his craft in Alabama. He was managing a slash-and-burn campaign for Harold See, a Republican running for a seat on the state Supreme Court.

See's opponent was incumbent Mark Kennedy, a moderate Democrat who was also the son-in-law of George Wallace. Kennedy was widely respected in the state, not only for his work on the court, but for his long and consistent advocacy for abused children. As the *Atlantic* noted in a profile of Rove, Kennedy was a founder of the Children's Trust Fund of Alabama and the Corporate Trust Fund for Children. At the time he was running for reelection he had just served a term as president of the National Committee to Prevent Child Abuse and Neglect. His campaign ads touted this work. One contained an image of Kennedy holding hands with children. Rove responded with a whisper campaign—carried out by conservative law students at the University of Alabama—that Kennedy was a homosexual pedophile.

"One of Rove's signature tactics is to attack an opponent on the very front that seems unassailable," wrote Joshua Green in the *Atlantic*. "Kennedy was no exception." Kennedy won reelection in 1994. He decided it would be his last term.

THAT SAME POST-COLD-WAR SAVAGERY so evident in presidential campaigns infected Congress with the rise of a young Republican bomb thrower named Newt Gingrich. The state of Georgia unleashed Gingrich on the nation, although he was actually born in Pennsylvania and spent his childhood moving around as his mother followed his stepfather, who was in the military. Gingrich attended Tulane University for his doctorate in history and while there decided to move to a semi-rural district in Georgia to pursue his political ambitions, according to a 1995 profile in the *New Yorker*. Writer Connie Bruck describes a narcissistic hypocrite with overweening ambition—Donald Trump, but with a higher IQ.

A history and geography professor at what is now the University of West Georgia in Carrollton, Gingrich told colleagues that he planned to become Speaker of the U.S. House of Representatives. That was before he won election to Congress, or to any other political office, for that matter. "Bright, not brilliant," according to one of his professors, Gingrich was hardly a natural politician. He was arrogant, disdainful, didactic. But on his third try, in 1978, he won election to Georgia's Sixth Congressional district.

Many who had supported Gingrich in his early Congressional campaigns were surprised—and disappointed—when he made a hard turn to the right. At first, he had campaigned as a proud Rockefeller Republican, supporting environmental and civil rights causes. But his ideology was nothing if not fungible. In 1975, Bruck writes, he attended a campaign strategy seminar run by the right-wing activist Paul Weyrich (who would become a decades-long adviser) and another ultra-conservative strategist, J. Frederic Rench. A GOP donor told Bruck, "It was with Rench and Weyrich that Newt was energized to come to understand a lot about the political opportunities that were there for conservatives." And Weyrich took it upon himself to "make Newt a star of the conservative movement."

Weyrich needed Gingrich to help Republicans gain control of the U.S. House of Representatives, though he understood quite well that Gingrich had no enduring values other than self-advancement. Cultural conservatives emphasized marital fidelity, but Gingrich started an affair with a young woman named

Marianne Ginther shortly after he arrived in Washington, and he left his first wife, Jackie, to marry Ginther. When Jackie was still in the hospital recovering from surgery for cancer, Gingrich went to her room with a yellow legal pad to discuss the details of their divorce.

Still, always scheming his way to the top, Gingrich was named Minority Whip in 1989. He had gained notice among his colleagues when he launched an ethics investigation of Democratic House Speaker Jim Wright that ended Wright's tenure. But there was a significant obstacle standing between Gingrich and the speakership: even if Republicans won the House, his GOP colleagues were unlikely to support him because they didn't like him. Many thought he was a jerk. Back then, bi-partisanship was the oil that greased the wheels of Congress, making it possible to pass legislation. Old-fashioned institutionalists such as GOP Minority Leader Bob Michel were upset by Gingrich's personal attacks on Democrats.

Gingrich solved that problem by launching a years-long effort to elect a new cohort of Republicans to Congress who would be intensely loyal to him. From his perch as head of the Republican political training organization, Gingrich not only helped to fund would-be congressmen but also told candidates what issues and messages they should use on the campaign trail. He urged the use of cultural issues to anger and energize white conservatives, so he taught Republican candidates to emphasize crime and welfare dependency.

A student of warfare, Gingrich believed that politics should employ similar strategies, including de-humanizing the enemy. He ran campaign seminars and issued audio tapes teaching

Republicans to use incendiary rhetoric to describe Democrats, fellow Americans though they were. "Sick," traitors," "corrupt," bizarre," "cheat," "steal," "devour," and "self-serving" were among the adjectives and nouns he recommended. Gingrich is also credited with teaching Republicans to drop the "ic" from the adjective form of the name of their party's rival, so that Republicans still say "Democrat Party," abusing the English language. Gingrich believed that referring to colleagues across the aisle as "Democratic" gave them too much credit (although the GOP's increasing turn to autocracy reveals much about its own principles). In any case, as Weyrich told Bruck, "We decided we had to learn to frame issues so as to seize the moral high ground; we had to develop better systems of communication; we had to learn to nationalize campaigns."

In 1994, Gingrich was elected speaker with the loyal support of his acolytes. The malicious language used against Democrats became commonplace, eventually infecting the Senate as Gingrich disciples such as former Pennsylvania senator Rick Santorum moved to the upper chamber. The scorched-earth tactics, most notably used to impeach President Bill Clinton, became commonplace as well.

Gingrich was ultimately brought low by his arrogance and hypocrisy. Though he was in the middle of his own extramarital affair with the woman who would become his third wife, he helped to whip up the frenzy over Clinton's extramarital relationship with Monica Lewinsky, assuring his partisans that impeaching Clinton was a winning issue. It was not. Though the GOP maintained control of the House, the party lost seats. House Republicans revolted, and Gingrich stepped down from his leadership position. Pouting, he resigned from Congress a few weeks later.

That virtually ended his political career. He sought the Republican nomination for the presidency in 2012 but made a poor showing. Still, he had left his awful mark on American politics. Bitter polarization, the combativeness and crude insults that now characterize Republican political rhetoric and the tactics of obstruction, including stand-offs over paying the nation's debts, are Gingrich's legacy.

THERE IS ONE MORE ingredient in this story of political decline—this story of a new toxicity in the political life of the nation. Early in the new millennium, one of its shrines stood sentinel off Interstate 85 just north of the gleaming skyline of Charlotte. Northside Baptist was the city's first megachurch. Its founding minister, Jack Hudson, stalked the pulpit of his domed sanctuary, often overflowing with thirty-four hundred or more of the faithful. He was a bombastic man, both in sermons and private interviews, and in the 1970s he was one of the leaders of the anti-busing movement. He started a Christian school at his church, which served grades kindergarten through twelve. All its students were white.

Hudson retired in 1990, and Dan Burrell, the second in the line of his successors, was a man with a different personality and message. "The Scriptures scream racial unity," he said. The Northside school was now open to all races. But if Burrell was genial and self-effacing—"left to my own devices," he declared, "I'll be a disaster; the only hope I have is what Christ has done through me"—he shared with Hudson a belief in "the absolute authority of the Scriptures." He also shared a propensity for political activism, with segregation now replaced as an issue by homosexuality and abortion. And he saw little reason to search for common ground.

"Compromise," he conceded, "is the lifeblood of politics, but the death knell of theology . . . I believe I am fighting for eternal truths."

It was one of the peculiarities of the late twentieth century that this evangelical certainty—"I am right and you are wrong, and there is nothing for us to talk about"—became intertwined with the Republican habit of winning. From Reagan's dispatch of Jimmy Carter, which solidified the partisan transformation of the South, through Bush's win over Michael Dukakis, the GOP controlled the presidency for twelve straight years. There was, it seemed, a fierce entitlement that went with that success. In the Republican rage following the victories of Bill Clinton—the flawed, charismatic former Arkansas governor, so gifted at framing the public debate—politics became more than ever the great blood sport of American life.

In all of this, there were those who believed—with a blinding righteousness sometimes spilling into hate—that God, most surely, was on their side.

Traumas of the New Millennium

FRYE GAILLARD

The calendar turned with a proclamation of hope, coming from the President of the United States. In the closing years of his administration, Bill Clinton spoke of "building a bridge to the twenty-first century," which seemed to be, as he understood it, a time of possibility and promise. As a Southern politician who came of age in the civil rights years, Clinton had a gift for messaging—for recasting the rhetoric of social justice in a way that Americans found persuasive.

On January 27, 2000, he declared in his final State of the Union: "To twenty-first-century America, let us pledge these things: Every child will begin school ready to learn and graduate ready to succeed. Every family will be able to succeed at home and at work, and no child will be raised in poverty . . . We will assure quality, affordable health care, at last, for all Americans. We will make America the safest big country on Earth . . ."

Clinton could boast of economic progress—twenty million new jobs, the lowest unemployment rate in thirty years, the lowest poverty rate in twenty, and perhaps most remarkably, a federal budget surplus two years in a row. But this was a speech of famous last words, rendered so ironic in the coming months—and certainly in the next twenty years—that it sounded almost like political satire: "We are fortunate to be alive in this moment in history. Never before has our Nation enjoyed, at once, so much prosperity and social progress with so little internal crisis and so few external threats."

Part of the irony was Clinton's own failing, for among the flaws in his presidency were issues of character—sexual appetites he failed to control, which not only led to his impeachment but fed the partisan bloodlust of his political enemies. The latter had a life of its own. In the end, Clinton deepened divisions he wanted to oppose, and in the years that followed, everything would get much worse.

INDEED, THE FIRST ELECTION in the new millennium was not only bitterly fought and close, but it was decided ultimately by one of the most partisan rulings—deliberately or not—in the modern history of the U.S. Supreme Court.

Not that *Bush v. Gore* was an easy case, as even its harshest critics had to admit. In this presidential contest between two Southerners—one the son of a president, the other of a senator, each his father's namesake—the final result came down to Florida. Vice President Al Gore, a Democrat running to succeed his boss, was leading nationally in the popular vote (by a margin of 543,895). But in the anachronisms of the Electoral College, if George W. Bush could cling to his lead in Florida, he would win the presidency. It was razor thin. After an automatic recount, Bush was ahead by 317 votes. The Gore campaign asked for a manual recount, and that was when America learned of "hanging chads."

Multiple counties in Florida had used punch-card ballots, and some voters had failed to fully punch out the paper tab, or chad, beside the name of their candidate, leaving it to election officials to determine whether the ballot should count. In ordering a manual re-tabulation, the state Supreme Court offered instructions both sensible and vague—that the counters seek to discern "the clear intent of the voter." The Bush campaign appealed that ruling to the U.S. Supreme Court, which stopped the recount and essentially handed the election to Bush. The Court's final ruling was decided 5–4, though the justices agreed more broadly on the problem. Because of inconsistencies in the count—which chads were "hanging," and which merely "dimpled," and how could anybody be sure of "intent?"—seven justices saw a pattern of disparate treatment, which represented a violation of the Equal Protection Clause of the Constitution.

There was a 4–4 split over what to do about it. The conservatives on the court—Republicans all—voted to end the count where it stood, precisely at a time when the conservative Republican running for president was still in the lead. Liberals wanted to extend the process—until January if that's what it took—seeking the most accurate possible result. The swing vote fell to Sandra Day O'Connor, the court's first woman justice, who had played a decisive role before. During the nineteen years since her appointment by President Reagan, O'Connor had cast the deciding vote in *Grutter v. Bollinger*, upholding affirmative action in higher education, and *Planned Parenthood of Southern Pennsylvania v. Casey*, which preserved the precedent of *Roe v. Wade*. Her integrity was a matter of record.

But there was also this. O'Connor, a Republican, had told family and friends that she was planning to retire if a member of her party won the presidential election. Did this aspiration, even subconsciously, play a role in her decision? As historian

Erin Blakemore wrote, "There is no way to know . . ." But the appearance of partisanship was there, and O'Connor knew it. She continued to agonize about her role, wondering if the court should have considered the case at all.

In 2013, she told an interviewer with the *Chicago Tribune*, "Maybe the court should have said, 'We're not going to take it, goodbye.'"

The damage, however, was done. The taint of partisanship was present, a wound to public trust that has not yet healed—that in fact has been frequently reopened and has only grown more toxic over time. "Although we may never know with complete certainty the identity of the winner of this year's Presidential election," wrote Justice John Paul Stevens in his *Bush v. Gore* dissent, "the identity of the loser is perfectly clear. It is the Nation's confidence in the judge as an impartial guardian of the rule of law."

As soon as he took the oath of office, President Bush did what he could to repair the damage. In his inaugural address he offered a unifying theme, a portrait of what his father might have called a "kinder, gentler America," with all its possibilities and flaws. Even some of us who voted against Bush had to be impressed—had to admit to a flicker of approval—as we watched his performance on our television sets. Bush declared:

> While many of our citizens prosper, others doubt the promise, even the justice, of our own country. The ambitions of some Americans are limited by failing schools and the circumstances of their birth. And sometimes our differences run so deep, it seems we share a continent, but not a country. We do not accept this,

and we will not allow it. Our unity, our union, is the serious work of leaders and citizens in every generation. And this is my solemn pledge: I will work to build a single nation of justice and opportunity.

It was hard to know what to make of such a speech. Certainly, the words sounded healing at a time of partisanship on the rise. But did Bush really mean it? The evidence was mixed. He had appointed General Colin Powell as his Secretary of State, an African American and moderate Republican who was one of the most respected figures in the country. But there were contra-indications—conservative hard-liners like Vice President Dick Cheney and Defense Secretary Donald Rumsfeld, who would be making their demands on the president's ear.

Who would prevail?

SOON ENOUGH THE ANSWER was clear, and it came in a way that few imagined—in a moment that even now sends ripples of dread through the heart of the country, more subtly perhaps, but more profoundly than even its perpetrators might have dreamed.

For some of us, 9/11 brought back memories of the 1960s. Just as we could remember where we were and what we were doing when President John Kennedy was assassinated—or Dr. King, or RFK—time stopped again when we saw the planes fly into the towers. Most of us were watching on television, as first one plane and then a second were transformed into bombs, exploding with diabolical force into the symbols of America's economic might.

In his Pulitzer Prize-winning book, *The Looming Tower:*

Al-Qaeda and the Road to 9/11, Texas-born journalist Lawrence Wright described a scene that was being replayed again and again as we tried to fathom what had happened to the country:

> The cloudless sky filled with coiling black smoke and a blizzard of paper—memos, photographs, stock transactions, insurance policies—which fluttered for miles on a gentle southeasterly breeze, across the East River into Brooklyn. Debris spewed onto the streets of lower Manhattan, which were already covered with bodies. Some of them had been exploded out of the building when the planes hit. A man walked out of the towers carrying someone else's leg . . . By now, the first jumpers had broken through the windows of the north tower above the burning jet fuel. Their flailing bodies landed like grenades.

In a masterpiece of reporting, Wright traced the twisted evolution of jihad, an ideology that ironically had first gained momentum near the scene of the crime. Before Osama bin Laden, there was Sayyid Qutb, an Egyptian writer and educator who would become the martyred patron saint of radicals. In 1948, Qutb came to New York to study and was so appalled by the gaudy trappings of materialism that seemed to go with Western democracy—and worse, he thought, a kind of budding sexual freedom—that he found himself on a deeper dive into Islamic fundamentalism. Americans, he wrote, were "a reckless, deluded herd that only knows lust and money."

He began to dream about pure Islam as practiced in the days of the Prophet Mohammad—a medieval fantasy that slowly took hold in the tumult of the next fifty years. The Islamic world, as

Wright explains, was racked with disillusionment and shame, especially after the Six Day War when the nation of Israel—"the Jews of Palestine" in the contemptuous words of one Muslim radical—quickly repelled an attack by its neighbors, seizing additional Arab land in the process. This was 1967. A decade later, the Soviet Union invaded Afghanistan, and in 1982, with the tacit approval of the United States, Israel invaded Lebanon.

Osama bin Laden, who was then a rich young Saudi radicalized by these events, would recall his horror at the carnage in the city of Beirut: ". . . blood and severed limbs, women and children sprawled everywhere. Houses destroyed along with their occupants and high rises demolished over their residents . . . The situation was like a crocodile meeting a helpless child, powerless except for his screams."

With the eventual collapse of the Soviet Union, exhausted as it was by the deadly futility of its Afghan adventure, only the United States was left in bin Laden's personal pantheon of hate. He regarded America as a pitiful giant. As bin Laden understood it, despite their bluster and bellicose words, American presidents had quit the fight in Vietnam when the cost in blood had grown too high. Even more pathetically, in 1983, when suicide bombers struck the U.S. Embassy and Marine Corps barracks in Beirut, killing more than three hundred Americans, President Reagan immediately withdrew the U.S. peacekeeping force.

For the next twenty years, as bin Laden assembled an army of sociopaths, he had, in Wright's words,

> developed a fixed idea about America, which he explained to each new class of al-Qaeda recruits. America appeared so mighty,

he told them, but it was actually weak and cowardly. Look at Vietnam, look at Lebanon. Whenever soldiers start coming home in body bags, Americans panic and retreat. Such a country needs only to be confronted with two or three sharp blows, then it will flee in panic, as it always has. For all its wealth and resources, America lacks conviction. It cannot stand against warriors of faith who do not fear death.

The victory of Islam was at hand.

This was bin Laden's article of faith, his fever-dream understanding of God and the Prophet Mohammed and the Islamist radicals since Sayyid Qutb. All of it finally came to fruition on 9/11. "In Afghanistan," according to Wright, "bin Laden . . . wept and prayed. The accomplishment of striking two towers was an overwhelming signal of God's favor, but there was more to come. Before his incredulous companions, bin Laden held up three fingers." And another plane struck the Pentagon.

IN THE DAYS AND years that followed, most Americans cared little about these details. They had no interest in the intricacies of madness, for they were filled with rage and disbelief, a new feeling of vulnerability. And so they rallied behind a cowboy president. On September 14, three days after the attack, Bush began the day with an interfaith service at the Washington National Cathedral. There was an opening prayer by a Muslim cleric, Imam Muzammil Siddiqi, followed by "The Battle Hymn of the Republic," and a sermon by the Reverend Billy Graham. Journalists noted that the mood was "mostly somber."

After the service, the president boarded Air Force One and

flew to McGuire Air Force Base in New Jersey, then by helicopter to the wreckage of the World Trade Center. By now, he had changed to a gray shirt, open at the collar, and tan windbreaker. Robert McFadden of the *New York Times* described the scene at Ground Zero.

> Like many Americans, the president had seen pictures of the devastation where nearly five thousand people lay buried. Still, he seemed awed as he stared up at the slope of twisted steel and concrete that four days ago had been towers that dominated the Lower Manhattan skyline.
>
> Climbing atop a charred fire truck, draping his arm around a sixty-nine-year-old retired firefighter, Mr. Bush grabbed a bullhorn.
>
> "We can't hear you!" someone yelled.
>
> "I can hear you," the president bellowed back. "The rest of the world hears you, and the people who knocked these buildings down will hear all of us soon."
>
> "U.S.A.! U.S.A.! U.S.A.!" they chanted.

Soon, however, the mistakes began, each building upon the last, as Bush inevitably began to squander the national unity that was his for the taking. With prior authorization from Congress, he ordered the bombing of Afghanistan where the Taliban government of Islamic fundamentalists had allowed bin Laden to orchestrate his attacks. That alone might not have been a problem. Everybody knew that America would retaliate. Bush, however, also ordered in ground troops, ignoring powerful lessons of history going back to Alexander the Great and certainly to the Soviet invasion of the 1980s. It has become a cliché that Afghanistan, with its rugged terrain and fierce tribal fighters, is a place where powerful armies go to die.

And then it got worse. On March 19, 2003, the Bush Administration invaded Iraq. Rumsfeld, Cheney, and other hardliners were convinced that America's military might could reshape the Middle East in its own image. But amid the "shock and awe" of the bombing raids, which we could watch live on our television sets, and the mounting toll of civilian casualties, which we could not, it began to dawn on many that this was a war of choice, based on misinformation, or, less euphemistically, on lies. Iraq had not attacked us on 9/11, nor did its dictator, Saddam Hussein, admittedly a murderous man, have at his disposal the weapons of mass destruction the Administration had claimed. And soon we heard the stories of torture, saw the images from Abu Ghraib of the crimes being carried out in our names. Our unity of vulnerability and rage, forged in the terror of 9/11, began to come apart.

FROM THE START, THE unraveling was ugly and absurd. On March 10, 2003, as the war was looming but had not yet begun, Natalie Maines, a Texan and the lead singer for the country group the Dixie Chicks, told an overflow crowd in London: "Just so you know, we're on the good side with y'all. We do not want this war, this violence, and we're ashamed that the president of the United States is from Texas." As Brian Hiatt wrote in *Rolling Stone*, "For country-radio programmers, and at least a hysterical minority of fans, it was as if she'd French-kissed Saddam Hussein while setting fire to a puppy wrapped in the American flag." Right-wing commentators went crazy. On Fox News, Bill O'Reilly called the Chicks "callow, foolish women who deserve to be slapped around."

It all became an orchestrated response to what was arguably at the time the most popular country band in the world. The Dixie Chicks consisted of three Texas girls, Maines, Martie Maguire, and Emily Strayer, who sang of cowboys and wide-open spaces, and once more topically and tongue in cheek the murder of an abusive husband. On election night in 2000, they had played at a party for George W. Bush. But now they were banned by the corporate moguls of country radio and taunted by the voices on talk radio, on stations often owned by the same conglomerates. In a feeding frenzy of hate and disdain, there were death threats and public bonfires of Dixie Chick records. It was also true, as one country songwriter noted ironically, "A lot of those people had to buy the records to burn them. They were never fans in the first place."

Such was the unreality of the moment.

For one of the writers of this book, a measure of the collective lunacy came in a conversation with a neighbor. We were talking about the Dixie Chicks, and whether or not they hated America, and this farmer in rural North Carolina, who grew a little marijuana on the side, said he liked their songs well enough, but would never listen to them again.

"Wait a minute," said the writer. "They don't hate America. They just don't like the War in Iraq. They don't see why we're attacking a country that never did anything to us."

"Well," said the farmer, dropping his voice, "the way I figure, if you've seen one sand n-----, you've seen them all."

THERE IT WAS—THE RAW obscenity of dread, the fear and loathing that was sweeping through the land, making people crazy. In the presidential campaign of 2008, on an October day in Minnesota, Republican John McCain was speaking at a rally, a free-form discussion with his avid supporters, when one expressed grave fears about McCain's Democratic opponent: "My wife and I are expecting our first child, and frankly we're scared. We're scared of an Obama presidency."

McCain grimaced.

"I want to be president of the United States," he replied, sounding somber and firm, "and obviously I do not want Senator Obama to be. But I have to tell you—I have to tell you, he is a decent person, and a person that you do not have to be scared of as president of the United States."

The crowd booed. "Come on, John," one person yelled.

Another reached for the microphone. "I can't trust Obama," she declared, stammering, searching for words to describe her fear. "I have read about him and he's not . . . uh—he's an Arab."

"No, ma'am," McCain insisted, looking even more uncomfortable. "He's a decent family man [and] citizen that I just happen to have disagreements with on fundamental issues and that's what this campaign is about. He's not [an Arab]."

For McCain, it was a complicated moment. Sarah Palin, his vice presidential running mate, had been making the campaign uneasy, throwing around accusations about Obama "palling around with terrorists"—a debasement of the public debate that was not what McCain had in mind. But he had picked her, and in the rush to make that decision his campaign staff had failed in its vetting. Now they were reaping what they had sown, becoming part of a national hysteria that was, as McCain would later admit, "not the kind of campaign I wanted to run."

On October 10, 2008, he was doing what he could to repair the damage. Political pundits, even Obama himself, praised his statesmanship, but it was also clear in the gloom of that day that people in the crowd were not convinced. They had little interest in civility or nuance. They were frightened. Some were spoiling for a fight. To make matters worse from their point of view, Barrack Obama won the election.

In all the interwoven division, fear, and mounting partisanship and paranoia of the new millennium, there may have been nothing more surprising than the national reaction to the first black president. At first, it seemed to be a fine thing. Civil rights leaders wept for a dream deferred. Massive crowds gathered for Obama's inauguration, and political commentators began to speculate about a new era in American history—a moment of irreversible progress.

But others were not so sure.

"I was baffled by national pundits declaring a post-racial America because a black man was in the White House," remembered Isaac Bailey, an African American former newspaper columnist and now a professor at Davidson College in North Carolina. "What I saw was white neighbors, friends and colleagues clinging more passionately to their racial identity."

"The symbolism of Obama's election," said political scientist Ashley Jardina of Duke University, "was a profound loss to whites' status."

In her runaway bestseller, *Caste*, Pulitzer Prize-winner Isabel Wilkerson argued that only a freakish confluence of circumstance had led to Obama's election in the first place. The original ingredient was the star power of the candidate himself— "the human equivalent of a supernova," she said.

> . . . a Harvard-trained lawyer, a U.S. senator from the land of Lincoln, whose expertise was the Constitution itself, whose charisma and oratory matched or exceeded that of most any man who had ever risen to the Oval Office, whose unusual upbringing inclined him toward conciliation of the racial divide, who famously saw the country not as blue states or red states but as the United States, whose wife, if it could be imagined, was also a Harvard-trained lawyer with as much star power as her husband, who, together with their two young daughters, made for a telegenic American dream family, and who, beyond all this, ran a scrupulous, near-flawless campaign, a movement really. It would take an idealist, who believed what most Americans would have sworn was impossible, for a black man to make it to the White House.

Add to McCain's flawed campaign what Wilkerson called "a once-in-a-generation financial catastrophe"—which led not only to the collapse of Wall Street but to plunging values of American homes—and Obama was able to win the presidency. But 57 percent of white voters opposed him. In 2012, when he won reelection, his share of the white vote dropped to 39 percent.

Far from being a sign that the issue of race was in the past, Obama's victories, polarizing from the start, summoned old demons in a way Americans did not see coming. The opposition party refused to work with Obama at all. "The single most important thing we want to achieve," said Senate Majority Leader Mitch McConnell, a Kentucky Republican, "is for President Obama to be a one-term president." The partisan rigidity quickly embraced a startling abandonment of decorum—Republican Representative Joe Wilson of South Carolina shouting out, "You lie," as Obama addressed a joint session of Congress; Republican Governor Jan Brewer of Arizona jabbing her finger at Obama's face in a conversation at the Phoenix airport. (As Wilkerson noted, the president appeared "calm and stoic, if slightly bemused.")

And there were the lies. Sarah Palin, who played a willful role in untethering her political party from the truth, coined the phrase "death panel" in a Facebook post about Obama's proposed health care reforms. On August 7, 2009, when the Affordable Care Act was still being drafted, Palin wrote: "The America I know and love is not one in which my parents or my baby with Down Syndrome will have to stand in front of Obama's 'death panel' so his bureaucrats can decide, based on a subjective judgment of their 'level of productivity in society.'" No such panels were being proposed. But talk radio echoed Palin's insinuation.

"She's dead right," said Rush Limbaugh.

For the growing army of right-wing pundits, it was as if there were something so alien—so self-evidently un-American—about Obama that they were freed of any obligation to the truth. Soon enough, the undisputed master of such innuendo was a reality television host who was beginning to consider, in 2011, the possibility of running for president.

As ASHLEY PARKER REPORTED in the *Washington Post*, Donald Trump was not the inventor of "birtherism," the suggestion that the country's first black president was not born in the United States. But Trump became increasingly obsessed with the issue as one that might raise his profile during his first presidential dalliance. He discovered that it worked—particularly when he tied innuendo about Obama's birth to the possibility that he was a Muslim. "He doesn't have a birth certificate," Trump told Fox News. "He may have one, but there is something on that birth certificate—maybe religion, maybe it says he's a Muslim; I don't know." A few weeks later, in April 2011, he hinted darkly to NBC, "I have people that have been studying it and they cannot believe what they are finding."

With the echo chamber of the national media, particularly Fox, but other more mainstream outlets as well, Obama eventually felt obliged to release his long-form birth certificate demonstrating conclusively that he was born in Hawaii. You could almost see his eye-rolling. "I was pretty sure where I was born," he said. By then, however, more than half of Republican voters had become convinced that Obama was not born in America. Trump, though he eventually did not run in 2012, filed the lesson away.

Isabel Wilkerson would soon make the case that this was the caste system swinging into action—the American iteration of an ancient idea, with roots running deep in the American South. Some people were just *born better* than others. That was the fundamental premise. Wilkerson quoted multiple contemporaneous sources who justified the institution of slavery—and its heirs in the era of Jim Crow—with proclamations of white supremacy as the God-given order of things.

Alexander Stephens, vice president of the Confederacy, had said of his new secessionist state:

Its foundations are laid, its cornerstone rests, upon the great truth that the negro is not equal to the white man; that slavery, subordination to the superior race, is his natural and moral condition. This, our new Government, is . . . based upon this great physical, philosophical, and moral truth. . . . With us, all of the white race, however high or low, rich or poor, are equal in the eye of the law. Not so the negro. Subordination is his place. He, by nature, or by the curse of Canaan, is fitted for that condition which he occupies in our system.

Wilkerson maintains that this assumption, sometimes less venomously stated, never really disappeared from the American psyche and began, in fact, to make a comeback in 2008. Two things happened that year. First, the U.S. Census Bureau issued a prediction that by 2042—not that far in the future—whites would no longer make up a majority of Americans; a plurality, yes, but no longer a majority capable of imposing its will. And then, as if to illustrate the possibility, a black man was elected president.

"I went to bed last night," lamented Rush Limbaugh, after Obama was reelected in 2012, "thinking we're outnumbered. I went to bed last night thinking we've lost the country. I don't know how else you look at this."

As WILKERSON NOTED, THE fears that Limbaugh put into words led to measures more concrete than a pundit's bombast. As Tea Party Republicans vowed to "take our country back," the GOP began changing election laws, making it harder to vote. Only two years before Obama's election, President Bush had signed an extension of the Voting Rights Act that passed overwhelmingly in the U.S. House of Representatives and unanimously in the U.S. Senate. The right to vote was a bipartisan truth, touted by a Republican president as one of his cornerstone commitments. But no longer. On June 25, 2013, in a case coming out of Alabama, the U.S. Supreme Court gutted key provisions of the Voting Rights Act, and in the next three years nearly sixteen million people were deleted from voter registration lists.

Meanwhile, there was hatred in the air. Social media posts compared the President and First Lady to monkeys and apes, armed participants at political rallies carried signs proclaiming "Death to Obama"; and one day during the birther controversy, a man parked his car on Constitution Avenue and began firing his semiautomatic rifle toward the upper floors of the White House—toward the rooms where the First Family lived. A bullet lodged in the windowsill. (The shooter is in federal prison, slated to be released in 2033.)

But perhaps most ominously, as a measure of the free-floating rage, by 2015 police were killing unarmed African Americans at five times the rate of whites—at a rate that was a disturbing reminder of the rate of lynching in the Jim Crow era. Obama took some of this in stride. When it came to the insults hurled in his direction, or even the intransigence of the opposition party, one of his seminal achievements as president may have been simply that he kept his cool; more than that, he remained a symbol of dignity and grace. But as Michelle Obama wrote in *Becoming*, her best-selling memoir, the reality of violence hit close to home. She described her thoughts as the Obama presidency was moving toward an end.

For more than six years now, Barack and I had lived with an awareness that we ourselves were a provocation. As minorities across the country were gradually beginning to take on more significant roles in politics, business, and entertainment, our family had become the most prominent example. Our presence in the White House had been celebrated by millions of Americans, but it also contributed to a reactionary sense of fear and resentment among others. The hatred was old and deep and as dangerous as ever.

The occasion for these reflections was another mass shooting, the kind of event that was fast becoming normal. There had been such shootings before. Some of us remembered a day in 1966 when Charles Whitman, a former Marine with a brain tumor the size of a pecan, began firing randomly from a tower at the University of Texas. But it was also true that ever since the planes flew into the World Trade Center, violence on a terrifying scale was now a staple in American life—some might say, an addiction. It began this time after a twenty-one-year-old white man—a stranger—was invited to pray with a group of African Americans in Charleston. The date was June 17, 2015. Dylann Roof sat with the prayer group at Emanuel AME Church for nearly an hour before he pulled out a gun and started shooting. He killed nine people.

For President Obama, these were excruciating occasions. Official White House photographer Pete Souza remembered the December morning in 2012—shortly after his reelection—when news arrived that a gunman had killed twenty-six people at Sandy Hook Elementary School in Connecticut. "The

President slumped in reaction against the Oval sofa," Souza wrote in *Obama: An Intimate Portrait*. "He would come to say that it was the worst day of his presidency."

IN SOME RESPECTS, JUNE 26, 2015, was a different day. It began with the news that the U.S. Supreme Court upheld the right of same-sex couples to marry—an idea that Obama had endorsed as president—and that same night, the White House was lit in rainbow colors. But this was also the day he delivered the eulogy for the dead at "Mother Emanuel" church. It was a day he reflected on history and grace—on the founding of the church in 1817, and its role for black Americans in Charleston; how it was burned and then rebuilt and became a stop "for the weary along the Underground Railroad;" and then more recently how it was the safe harbor where the Reverend Clementa Pinckney, one of the casualties of Roof's rampage, had preached his powerful sermons on grace.

"I've been thinking a lot about grace," Obama said. "Blinded by hatred, the alleged killer would not see the grace surrounding Reverend Pinckney and that Bible study group, the light of love that shone as they opened the church doors and invited a stranger to join in their prayer circle . . . If we can find that grace, anything is possible. If we can tap that grace, everything can change." This was Obama's affirmation before he bit his lip and, after a pause, began to sing a cappella: "Amazing grace, how sweet the sound."

But was it true?

Were things he spoke about in Charleston—the mystical truths of love and grace that felt so alive as he sang the old hymn—really a match for the forces of violence? For the power of the National Rifle Association? After the trauma of every mass shooting, Wayne LaPierre, the NRA's executive vice president, inevitably stepped forward to proclaim that any additional gun regulation would mean the end of the Second Amendment. "What people all over the country fear," he declared after Sandy Hook, "is being abandoned by their government, if a tornado hits, if a hurricane hits, if a riot occurs, that they're going to be out there alone, and the only way they're going to protect themselves, in the cold, in the dark, when they're vulnerable, is with a firearm."

Eugene Robinson, Pulitzer Prize-winning columnist for the *Washington Post,* a South Carolinian who was old enough to remember when the NRA supported gun *safety*, argued that under LaPierre it had finally overplayed its hand. The organization had become so toxic that most Americans would inevitably recoil. Indeed, the NRA declared bankruptcy in 2021. But the damage was already done. Despite the self-evident absurdity of the NRA's message—that guns were making America safer—among a substantial minority of citizens the gun culture had taken deep root. The killing continued, and the country became more afraid.

And more willing to believe in lies.

The Golden Escalator

Frye Gaillard

On June 16, 2015, Donald Trump descended the golden escalator at Trump Tower in Manhattan to announce that he was running for president. It was a grand and ostentatious entrance that some of his advisers had warned him against. But Trump insisted. As he would demonstrate for the next five years, his sense of showmanship was finely tuned. With Melania Trump a few steps behind him, he smiled and waved at the cheering crowd—"padded with paid extras," as NBC's Katy Tur would report—and explained his reasons for seeking the office.

"When Mexico sends its people," he said in a voice dripping with disdain, "they're not sending their best . . . They're sending people with lots of problems, and they're bringing those problems with us. They're bringing drugs. They're bringing crime. They're rapists. And some, I assume are good people."

He promised he would build a wall to keep them out.

At first it was hard to take this in. Trump had never been elected to anything. He was a real estate mogul of dubious ethics, famous, if you could call it that, for a reality show on television that many people watched with the same bemusement—the same suspension of disbelief—that they might bring to professional wrestling (which Trump had dabbled in as a promoter). And now here he was, a candidate for president, dismissing Mexican immigrants as criminals and rapists, tarring them with a brush so broad that it could only be seen as racist.

How could he be running for president? He couldn't be serious, could he? It had to be some kind of hustle—a flight of ego perhaps? A scam to promote his real estate interests?

In the days that followed, things only got worse, at least by political norms if you assumed that Trump was trying to win. For one thing, he insulted U.S. Senator John McCain, a maverick member of his own party, who, whatever you might think of his views, was a war hero whose bravery and sacrifice in Vietnam were beyond all dispute. On October 26, 1967, McCain was flying his Skyhawk bomber at five hundred miles per hour above Hanoi when a missile the size of a telephone pole knocked the right wing off his plane. As the aircraft began to spin, McCain ejected from the cockpit, breaking both arms and his right leg as he did so. He landed in the middle of a lake and sank. Somehow he managed to swim to shore, despite his injuries and fifty pounds of gear. He was taken prisoner and held for more than five years, including two years of solitary confinement. He was tortured and beaten savagely, but he refused an early release because others had been in captivity even longer.

Incredibly, Donald Trump mocked him. In an interview only a short time after his golden escalator moment, Trump, who famously had avoided military service, insisted: "I prefer heroes who were not captured." From the vantage point of Alabama, this was an astonishing statement. We had our own Vietnam hero, Jeremiah Denton, who was also a POW in Hanoi and would later join McCain in the Senate. During a propaganda film the

North Vietnamese forced him to make, Denton blinked the word T-O-R-T-U-R-E, using Morse code with his eyes. These were brave men, deeply admired in the South and other parts of the heartland, and here was a candidate—a contemporary who had used bone spurs as an excuse to dodge Vietnam—jeering at their sacrifice for the country. Surely, Trump's candidacy was doomed.

But then he came to Alabama. On August 21, he spoke in Mobile at a rally that filled a football stadium. Official estimates put the crowd at more than fifteen thousand. The Trump campaign claimed thirty thousand, slightly more than had just turned out to hear Bernie Sanders in Los Angeles. Whatever the truth, the event was giddy—a testament to Trump and his showmanship that began with a late afternoon flyover in the campaign plane, while down below a tailgate party filled the parking lot; grills were smoking, vendors hawked Trump merchandise, and the candidate entered the stadium to the hard-rocking strains of "Sweet Home Alabama." A woman in the middle of the surging throng held up a hand-lettered sign with a curious pattern of capitalization: Thank You, Lord JESUS, FOR PRESIDENT TRUMP.

"That event was emblematic of what the Trump campaign ended up being," said Steve Taylor, a political scientist at Troy University. There was no indication that anybody worried about McCain.

Then and later Trump talked a lot about trade deals and weak politicians, but the heart of his message was always immigration—and a wall that Mexico would pay for. And the mood grew dark. Katy Tur of NBC had left an overseas assignment in London to cover a campaign that at first seemed like it might be a joke, but now, most assuredly, was not. On December 7, 2015,

Pearl Harbor Day, Trump moved into new territory. Following a mass shooting in San Bernardino, California in which the suspects were ISIS sympathizers, CNN reported with palpable astonishment: "Republican presidential front-runner Donald Trump called Monday for barring all Muslims from entering the United States . . . 'until our country's representatives can figure out what is going on.'" And as Tur reported, Trump doubled down at a rally that night in South Carolina, adding a bit of salty language for emphasis: ". . . until our country's representatives can figure out *what the hell* is going on."

Pundits and foreign policy experts, even his Republican rivals, recoiled in horror. Trump was talking, after all, about the second largest religion on earth—more than 1.6 billion people. "This is just more of the outrageous divisiveness that characterizes his every breath," said John Kasich, ". . . another reason why he is entirely unsuited to lead the United States." But the rally-goers loved it. One supporter, a soldier who had done tours in Iraq and Afghanistan, called on Trump to go even further.

"Ship them all back," he said.

All of this happened after a rally in Birmingham where a black protester interrupted Trump and was hauled away by security. The protester fell and a group of Trump supporters, all white, moved in to punch and kick him. The next day Trump said the demonstrator was obnoxious. "Maybe he should have been roughed up," he added. By the end of the year, the new Republican front-runner was musing about torture—waterboarding America's enemies because, he said, "they deserve it"—and about allegations that Vladimir Putin sometimes ordered the murder of journalists.

"I'd never kill them," Trump said at a Christmastime rally. "I hate them, but I would never kill them." The candidate paused and added with a smirk, as if to make certain the emphasis was clear: "But I do hate them." Tur, who was a frequent target of Trump's public wrath, later wrote in her memoir, *Unbelievable*, "Yes, we give Trump a ton of airtime and article space. But that's because he is unlike anything anyone has ever seen."

Except maybe George Wallace.

In 1964, and again in 1968, Wallace also pushed the boundaries of presidential discourse. He entered three primaries in 1964, startling pundits and leaders in both parties by winning substantial minorities of the vote. In 1968, he returned to the trail as a third-party candidate, a fact that terrified Richard Nixon, the Republican nominee, who had embarked on a "Southern strategy" of veiled racism. In the days leading up to the Republican Convention, Nixon had promised party leaders in the South that if he became president, neither he nor his Justice Department would rush to "satisfy some professional civil rights group, or something like that."

As historian Dan Carter noted in his book, *The Politics of Rage*, George Wallace was a little more blunt. With regard to officials in the federal government, he said he would "take those bearded bureaucrats and throw them in the Potomac." It soon became clear that millions of Americans preferred the real deal. Wallace began his campaign in the South, where a Baptist minister in Chattanooga proclaimed: "Outside the visible return of Jesus Christ, the only salvation of the country is the election of George Wallace." In Dallas, one of the warm-up speakers called him "America's divinely appointed savior."

At virtually every stop, the former governor drew standing ovations by conflating urban riots (prompted most often by police brutality) with "back-alley muggers" and urban crime. He wrapped the racial implications in code, adding bureaucrats, judges, and "out of touch politicians" to his cast of villains. Despite what his critics might want to believe, Wallace was a talented politician who offered his audience a transparent façade, easing the conscience even as blood began to boil. And it didn't take long for his recitations of grievance, tossed like pebbles in a Southern pond, to ripple powerfully to the nation as a whole.

"He tells it like it really is," said a steelworker in Youngstown, Ohio. "You don't have to worry about where he stands." From Hollywood, John Wayne made a thirty thousand dollar contribution with a one-sentence note: "Sock it to 'em, George." In a grassroots campaign fueled by small dollar donations (buckets literally passed through the crowds, sometimes netting thirty-five thousand dollars in a night), Wallace promised again and again to "Stand Up for America." His daughter, Peggy Wallace Kennedy, who would later emerge from her father's shadow to become a champion of civil rights in the South, acknowledged what the slogan really meant: "He was saying, stand up for white Southerners . . . for down-and-out white folks who had worked all their lives, gone to church on Sunday, and still took their hats off when the flag went by . . ."

The problem was, as with Trump a generation later, the scene turned dark. In her memoir, *The Broken Road*, Kennedy recalled her girl's-eye view of 1968: "The Wallace caravan moved from city to city. It had homespun humor and young girls prancing up and down the aisles with plastic donation buckets. It also had Wallace supporters with baseball bats."

At a July stop in Providence, Rhode Island, Wallace arrived at his hotel to find a small group of protesters waiting for him there. They were respectful. "Daddy," wrote Peggy, "made it a point to shake hands with each one."

But the rally that night was a different story.

> The crowd was large and anxious. Protesters unrolled banners and began to chant as Daddy rose to speak. He taunted them . . . telling them "All you hippies and pseudo-intellectuals are going to be through come election day. You use all those nasty four-letter words when you are talking about us. Well, how about these two for you, work and soap." Pointing to a male protester in the crowd, he would say, "You're a pretty little thing"—then, after a pause—"Oh my goodness, you're a he, not a she." And the crowds would roar.

It was an eerie foreshadowing of Trump—the dog whistles and taunting, the intimations of violence, even the similarity of their campaign slogans. But there was one major difference. In 1968, all of us knew that George Wallace would not be president. As Election Day approached in 2016, despite the polls and the certainty of pundits, a few reporters who had covered the race thought Trump had an excellent chance to win. Katy Tur was sure of it. So was the astute Gwen Ifill of PBS. Lawrence Wright, who spent his early career in Atlanta, covering the South for national magazines before becoming a staff writer at the *New Yorker*, would offer this post-mortem on Trump's 2016 triumph:

There was a singular genius at work, one that understood the American people better than we understood ourselves. Trump knew that, despite the pretense of morality nearly all candidates cling to, we are essentially a vulgar nation . . . He was brutish, cruel, and demeaning. . . . His opulent lifestyle was a cartoon of the American dream, but it dazzled, as did his appetite for attention. Another aspect of his genius was his near-magical ability to constantly turn people's heads in his direction, even if we hated ourselves for it; every day, every hour, every tweet, a new provocation arrived, and we stood there, like the knife-thrower's assistant as the blades flew, praying that the next one wouldn't be a mortal mistake. Still, how thrilling.

Some of us, particularly if we were raised in the Wallace South, thought it might be simpler than that. Yes, Trump was a bully and a showman, and there was something in us that gravitated to the menace. But much more significantly, Trump was a bigot, one who stoked a fear of Mexicans and Muslims as a prelude to a broader racism that he would normalize for the country. A lot of Americans—a minority that hovered around 40 percent—seemed happy about that. In any case, he won the election. The Golden Escalator continued its descent.

On January 20, 2017, the new administration began with a claim that Trump's inauguration crowd was bigger than President Obama's. As photographic evidence proved, it was not. At first this seemed like a silly distraction until we slowly began to realize that it was part of a concerted attack on reality. "Alternative facts" became an explanation offered by the president's top advisers—an intoxicating gift to his followers, who so often seethed with resentment and rage. Now, in giving voice to those feelings, they were free to say—*believe*—anything they wanted; the only test of truth was how loud and often they said it, and how good it felt when they did.

From there, the dystopia would deepen and spread. One week after his inauguration, Trump issued Executive Order 13769, his first attempt, broad and bumbling in its early iterations, to turn his Muslim ban into policy. He was persistent, issuing a second and then a third order after the first two were struck down by the courts. Eventually the U.S. Supreme Court ruled 5–4 in his favor. Meanwhile, Trump was assembling a team of like-minded advisers, and in the early days, one of the most important was Jeff Sessions, the junior senator from Alabama, picked to be his attorney general.

Sessions was already controversial. In 1986, after President Reagan nominated him for a federal judgeship, Coretta Scott King, among others, wrote a letter in opposition: "Mr. Sessions has used the awesome powers of his office in a shabby attempt to intimidate and frighten elderly black voters. For this reprehensible conduct, he should not be rewarded . . ." In 2017, during Sessions's confirmation hearings to be attorney general, Senator Elizabeth Warren attempted to read Mrs. King's letter into the record. Republican leaders refused to allow it. "Nevertheless, she persisted," lamented Majority Leader Mitch McConnell, who, inadvertently, with those three words, coined a new feminist slogan for the country.

Many Americans were simply confused. In the mainstream media, the Warren-McConnell dust-up appeared to be a partisan sideshow, always fuzzy, never fully explained. But to civil rights leaders, the backstory was chilling. In the 1980s, as a U.S. Attorney in Alabama, Sessions had brought federal charges against one of the icons of the movement. The case became known as "the Marion 3," after Sessions charged Albert Turner and two co-defendants with voter fraud. Turner was a provocative target. In 1965, he had emerged as a leader of the voting rights struggle in a part of Alabama where official opposition was violent and deadly. On February 18, 1965, Turner led a nighttime march in Marion after more than seven hundred young people were arrested in a voting rights demonstration. The students were driven like a herd of cattle to a high-walled stockade where they slept on a concrete floor and got their drinking water from a trough. At the same time, James Orange, a young organizer, was locked in solitary confinement in the Marion jail. There were rumors that the Klan would lynch him.

In response, Turner and his followers had begun a two-block march from a downtown church to the jail when they were attacked by the police. "Negroes could be heard screaming, and loud whacks rang through the square," wrote John Herbers of the *New York Times*. In the melee that followed, State Troopers were beating Cager Lee, an eighty-two-year-old farmer, when his grandson, Jimmie Lee Jackson, intervened. Jackson was a twenty-six-year-old army veteran and the youngest deacon at his small Baptist church. A state policeman shot him in the stomach.

Jackson's death was the trigger for the Selma to Montgomery March, and on Bloody Sunday, Albert Turner was on the second row, immediately behind John Lewis, as activists marched two-by-two across the Edmund Pettus Bridge. Three years later, in 1968,

Turner led the mule-drawn wagon that carried Dr. King's body to its grave. In 1985, this was the man Jeff Sessions went after.

As a U.S. Attorney, he charged Turner, his wife Evelyn, and another Alabama activist, Spencer Hogue, with conspiracy to commit voter fraud. According to the indictment, Turner and his fellow defendants had helped elderly African Americans fill out their absentee ballots, and some of the ballots had been altered. Evelyn Turner remembered her fear of hard prison time. She also remembered her dismay.

"We had always helped people with voting, for ages, and they trusted us," she told the *New York Times Magazine*. "Why would you mess with someone's ballot if you knew it wasn't what they wanted? We weren't fools."

A federal judge dismissed most of Sessions's case out of hand. A racially mixed jury, after deliberating for only four hours, found the defendants not guilty of the charges that remained. In a legal sense, Sessions had failed. But that may not have been the point.

"The trial took a toll," explained Mrs. Turner. "We had to sell our family's farm. I lost my job. The episode also took a toll on the voters of Perry County. The tactics of using the levers of power to intimidate and sow fear worked all too well. Black turnout dropped. People were afraid to exercise their constitutional right to vote for fear of retaliation backed by the power of the government. This was what Jeff Sessions did as a U.S. Attorney."

Partly because of such testimony, the Senate refused to confirm Sessions as a federal judge. But times change. In 2017, he was confirmed by a vote of 52–47 to be attorney general of the United States. For many of us in Alabama, who knew Sessions' record, this was a measure of racial change in the country—and certainly within the Republican Party.

It was not a measure of progress.

As attorney general, Sessions picked up where he had left off in the Senate. After his election to that body in 1996, he had vigorously applied his anti-civil rights sensibilities, which had worked well for him in Alabama, to the issue of immigration. In 2007, and again in 2013, as bipartisan compromise seemed to be in the air, Sessions set out to make sure it didn't happen. On the first occasion, senators Ted Kennedy and John McCain, strongly supported by President Bush, pushed for legislation that would have created a path to citizenship for some twelve million undocumented immigrants. The bill would have also bolstered border security. That was the basic compromise. Six years after those efforts failed, the U.S. Senate actually passed a similar bill with the backing of President Obama. The legislation died when Speaker John Boehner, a Republican, refused to allow a vote in the House.

Sessions was a bitter opponent of both attempts. When reform seemed possible, wrote Jonathan Blitzer in the *New Yorker*, "Sessions worked assiduously to scuttle it." In 2015, he circulated a memo entitled "Immigration Handbook for a New Republican Majority," urging his party to take a harder line. The following year, he could barely fathom his own good fortune when Trump won the election and picked him to be his attorney general. "It's really, really hard to believe," Sessions said. But he was determined to make the most of his opportunity.

"As the government's top lawyer," Blitzer concluded, he "was responsible for, among other things, . . . spurring family separations, trying to defund sanctuary cities, dismantling the asylum system, reshaping the immigration courts, and retooling multiple travel bans. To the extent that the President has styled himself as an anti-immigration crusader, it's with a script written entirely by Sessions." Most remarkably perhaps, if Trump in his Golden Escalator moment saw Mexican immigrants as "rapists," Sessions not only agreed, he regarded parents crossing the border with their children as smugglers. "If you are smuggling a child," he announced, "then we will prosecute you. That child will be separated from you as required by law." As the world soon learned, the attorney general meant it.

Among the signature cruelties of Donald Trump's agenda (another was Sessions' decision that a woman fleeing domestic abuse or a family escaping the terror of gangs were no longer eligible for asylum), family separation was a shock to the conscience. At least at first.

We learned about it on April 6, 2018, when Sessions announced a policy of "zero tolerance"—prosecuting every migrant who crossed the border illegally—and separating them from their children while they faced trial. Sessions had not consulted with other agencies, including Homeland Security, who would necessarily be involved in implementing the policy, but he knew the President loved the idea. He also knew that Trump despised him. Trump was furious about Sessions's decision to recuse himself from the Russia investigation, and the anger was deep and personal. (He referred to Sessions as a "dumb Southerner.") But the two men did share a passion for hardline immigration policy, and there was no harder line than this.

By the summer the policy had become controversial. Even

before Sessions announced it, there had been a blockbuster scoop in the *Houston Chronicle* about family separations in Texas. On April 20, the *New York Times* reported that more than seven hundred children had been taken from their parents along the whole southern border. The ACLU, meanwhile, had already filed its first case on behalf of a Congolese woman whose six-year-old daughter had been taken from her in San Diego and sent to a detention center in Chicago. In the *New York Review of Books* ACLU attorney Lee Gelerent described his first meeting with his client.

"Through a translator," he wrote, "she explained to the asylum lawyer and me that she feared for her and her daughter's lives, and that the Catholic Church helped them flee. They traveled through ten countries over four months, and requested asylum when they legally presented themselves" at an official port of entry. Nevertheless, Ms. L. was handcuffed and soon could hear her daughter screaming in fear, "Don't take me away from my mommy!"

On June 18, Homeland Secretary Kirstjen Nielsen was asked by the White House to defend the separation policy at a briefing with reporters. The press conference was a disaster. As Philip Rucker and Carol Leonnig reported in their book, *A Very Stable Genius*, Nielsen didn't know that *ProPublica* had just released tapes of children, aged four to ten, crying and pleading to see their parents. Leonnig and Rucker wrote:

> As Nielsen answered questions from reporters, Olivia Nuzzi of *New York* magazine played the recording aloud in the briefing room. In addition to the sounds of sniffling and cries of "Mami"

and "Papi," a six-year-old Salvadoran girl could be heard pleading to have someone call her aunt and repeating over and over the number she had memorized.

A Customs and Border Protection agent could be heard joking in a deep voice, "Well, we've got an orchestra here."

A reporter shouted out to Nielsen, "How is this not child abuse?"

Of all the news agencies that pursued this story, probably none were more dogged or less apologetic in their horror than the team at MSNBC. On June 19, the day after Nielsen's press conference, Rachel Maddow, near the end of her broadcast, began reading a report from the Associated Press. "This is incredible," she said. "Trump Administration officials have been sending *babies* and other young children to at least three . . ." Maddow stopped, teared up. She was suddenly unable to speak. She tried again, but choked on the words. "I think I'm going to have to hand this off. Sorry. That does it for us . . ." Later, she tweeted an apology: "Ugh, I'm sorry. If nothing else, it is my job to actually be able to speak while I'm on TV."

But this was an emotional story. Reporters Julia Ainsley and Jacob Soboroff took the lead on the network's coverage, and Soboroff later wrote a book, *Separated: Inside an American Tragedy.* He recounted the internal debate going back all the way to the Obama Administration, where a policy of family separation was considered and rejected. "I just couldn't do that," said Obama's Secretary of Homeland Security Jeh Johnson. But records show the practice began anyway. In the final months of 2016, with the Obama presidency winding down, more than one hundred families were separated by Border Patrol agents on the ground. The Trump Administration simply made it official.

Within the White House, the most unrelenting advocate for harsh deterrence was Stephen Miller, a policy adviser who came to the administration by way of Jeff Sessions. Miller, a graduate of Duke University, had worked for Sessions in the U.S. Senate. He first drew attention on the campaign trail with his blood-curdling stories of immigrant crime; one of the favorites was a murder committed by "a five-time deported illegal immigrant."

"Who the fuck is this dude?" wondered Soboroff. Soon he knew. In Trump's inner circle, Miller resolutely reinforced the president's instincts, as family separation became a fact of American life, and the reality of it began to sink in. On June 13, Soboroff flew to Brownsville, Texas, where he joined a small group of journalists who became the first to tour a detention facility. Some of the children he saw had come to the country by themselves. Others had been taken from their parents. No cameras were allowed inside, but Soboroff recounted what he saw: "This place is described as a shelter, but effectively these kids are incarcerated . . . People in here are locked up in cages, essentially what look like animal kennels. I don't know any other way to describe it."

Trump defenders soon countered that the same thing had happened under Obama. In fact, it had. Obama, who had deported more migrants than any other president, faced an unexpected crisis when unaccompanied children from Central America began to make the long, hazardous journey to the United States. They, too, were held in detention centers—often in similar cages—until other arrangements could be made. But there was now a massive difference in scale, compounded by the astonishing discovery that there was no plan to reunite the families. Many parents were being deported before that could happen. By the time the Biden Administration took office, more than a thousand migrant families still waited for their children to be returned.

In Geneva, the United Nations High Commissioner on Human Rights, Zeid Ra'ad Al Hussein, predicted that the separations would have "lifelong consequences." He urged the United States to ratify the Convention on the Rights of the Child.

Dr. Colleen Kraft, president of the American Academy of Pediatrics, remembered her 2018 visit to a children's detention center in Texas, where she saw a toddler sobbing, pounding her fists on a play mat: "She was just inconsolable. We all knew why she was crying. She was crying because she wanted her mother, and there was nothing we could do. This is something that was inflicted on this child by the government, and really is nothing less than government-sanctioned child abuse."

In protest, Steve Schmidt, who had managed John McCain's run for the presidency, resigned from the Republican Party. "This child separation policy is connected to the worst abuses of humanity in our history," he explained. "It is connected to the same evil that separated families during slavery and dislocated tribes and broke up Native American families. It is immoral . . . Our country is in trouble. Our politics are badly broken."

On a quiet downtown street in Montgomery, a brick warehouse with a long, dark history stands where it did before the Civil War—just a few blocks from the Alabama River and a railroad terminal that made Montgomery a hub in America's domestic slave trade. Literally thousands of enslaved men and women were unloaded on the docks, or from railroad cars, and herded up the street to the warehouse, where they were held awaiting sale. Not far away, but closer to the Capitol, historical markers record the spot where this human cargo was sold to plantation owners in the Alabama Black Belt, or in other parts of the deep South. Just up a hill, in the connected iconography of our place, a bronze star embedded in the marble floor of the Capitol portico marks where Jefferson Davis took his oath, and "Dixie" was played—for the first time—as the anthem of the Confederacy.

The old warehouse is also a memorial—a museum that opened in 2018, created by the Equal Justice Initiative to trace the through-line running from slavery to the present day: from the terrorism of lynching and the humiliations of racial segregation, to a criminal justice system that, among other things, creates a climate for police brutality. As soon as you walk through the door, you see on the wall the words of a man held captive here, recounting a particular moment of horror:

> I saw a mother lead seven children to the auction block. She knew some of them would be taken from her; but they took all. The children were sold to a slave trader. I met that mother in the street, and her wild, haggard face lives in my mind today. She wrung her hands in anguish and exclaimed, "Gone, all gone! Why don't God kill me?"

Preserving such history is not the only purpose of the EJI. Bryan Stevenson, the organization's founder, is a lawyer and author of the best-selling book, *Just Mercy: A Story of Justice and Redemption*. He spends much of his time working through a legal system he knows is flawed to oppose capital punishment and other harsh sentences—especially those imposed upon people on the margins of American life. But Stevenson also believes the nation must remember and reckon with the past—and because we have never mustered the will, we hear its echoes even now. There are few echoes more stark or elemental than the cries of children taken from their parents.

Steve Schmidt and other former Republicans worry that under the leadership of Donald Trump, their party began moving, not toward a reckoning, but resolutely in the opposite direction. Its golden escalator descended far beyond the issue of immigration, inflicting new wounds, stirring the ancient hatreds of race.

Black Lives Matter and Symbols of the Past

Cynthia Tucker

The massacre at Charleston's "Mother Emanuel" harkened back to the bloodiest days of the civil rights movement, when black girls at Sunday school could be blown to bits by savage racists. On June 17, 2015, nine worshippers, including the senior pastor, were shot to death during a Wednesday evening Bible study at a historic black church, Emanuel African Methodist Episcopal. Though all the more horrifying because the rampage was carried out on holy ground, it was followed by something resembling contrition—not from Dylann Roof, the culprit, but from the larger community that had acquiesced to his delusions. Admissions were made. Concessions were offered. White Southerners were forced to wrestle with the mythology of the Lost Cause, forced to acknowledge that the emblems and monuments of the Old Confederacy were not mere markers of heritage, as many among them insisted, but, for others, symbols of hate.

In a 2019 report on Confederate iconography across the nation, the Southern Poverty Law Center featured a 1951 quote from Georgia's Roy Harris, then editor of the *Augusta Courier:*

> The Confederate flag is coming to mean something to everybody now. It means the Southern cause. It is (coming) to be the

symbol of the white race and the cause of the white people. The Confederate flag means segregation.

Roof had certainly understood that. Among the photos he had carefully curated on social media were several in which he posed with the Confederate battle flag. After his arrest, he told police he wanted to start a race war.

South Carolina's Republican governor, Nikki Haley, daughter of immigrants, responded to Roof's rampage by calling for the removal of the Rebel flag from the grounds of the state capitol. She said:

> For many people in our state, the flag stands for traditions that are noble. Traditions of history, of heritage, and of ancestry . . . At the same time, for many others in South Carolina, the flag is a deeply offensive symbol of a brutally oppressive past.
>
> Fifteen years ago, after much contentious debate, South Carolina came together in a bipartisan way to move the flag from atop the Capitol dome. Today, we are here in a moment of unity in our state without ill will, to say it's time to move the flag from the Capitol grounds. A hundred and fifty years after the end of the Civil War, the time has come.

The canonization of the Confederacy as a noble Lost Cause began in earnest after Reconstruction, when white Southerners had won their political battle to expel federal troops from the region. But the campaign to build monuments and memorials took off decades after that, in the late nineteenth and early twentieth centuries, as the last veterans of the Civil War were dying off and family members and Southern historians wished to commemorate them and their presumed valor while defending the claimed rightness of their cause for which so much had been lost.

To do so, however, white Southerners needed to rewrite the history. They did not want to admit that enslaving fellow human beings was the central cause for such sacrifice. So they insisted that the Confederate states had rebelled against overweening Northern interference with states' rights; they populated their mythology with images of chivalrous Confederate officers, dainty but valiant Southern belles, and carefree, happy slaves.

That revisionist history was vigorously spread by the United Daughters of the Confederacy (UDC) and the United Sons of Confederate Veterans (SCV), formed in 1894–1896, through speech and essay contests, articles, letters, influence on textbooks, and more to teach "a proper respect for and pride in the glorious war history . . . and to perpetuate a truthful record of the noble and chivalric achievements of their ancestors." Both groups maintained Confederate cemeteries and raised funds for Confederate memorials that sprouted in public spaces around the South. Charter UDC member Helen Plane played a significant role in commemorating three Confederates—Jefferson Davis, Robert E. Lee and Thomas "Stonewall" Jackson—on Stone Mountain, just outside Atlanta. Sam Venable, owner of the granite outcropping, leased its north face to the UDC in 1916, and the UDC raised funds for what became the world's largest bas-relief sculpture, a massive depiction of the three men on horseback.

There is no excising the history of white terrorism from the Lost Cause: Venable had granted a group permission to burn a giant cross on the mountain in 1915 coincident with the release of the racist movie, *The Birth of a Nation*, and that event sparked the revival of the Ku Klux Klan that flourished over the next decade, when it gained more members, in both South and North, than it had in the Reconstruction era. Venable subsequently became an active Klansman; his nephew, James Venable, later became a KKK leader in Georgia in the 1960s–1980s. Lost Cause groups like the UDC and SCV retroactively gave cover to the terrorism of the original Ku Klux Klan, created in 1865 by six Confederate veterans, and then provided a genteel veneer to KKK violence in the 1920s, lynchings in the 1930s, and renewed KKK terrorism in the civil rights era.

As a native of Monroeville, Alabama, I can attest to the unthinking devotion to the Lost Cause of many white Southerners, who have been spoon-fed lies about the Civil War since infancy. During my childhood, Alabama's public school textbooks—as they did throughout the region—downplayed slavery, ignored it as the root cause of the Civil War, and spoke of a federal government that imposed unfair demands on the patriotic South before and after the war.

Across the South, flags emblazoned with the St. Andrew's cross and stars were ever-present above county courthouses and state capitols, on vehicle tags, on the shoulder patches and badges of state trooper and police uniforms, on the walls of private "seg academies," on T-shirts, caps, bumper stickers, flag poles and yard signs of private homes and businesses, and more. The Rebel battle flag has also been co-opted by white extremists since the 1950s. The symbol is as recognizable as the Coke bottle and, tellingly, the KKK hood and robe and burning cross.

Many all-white public schools ignored the national Memorial Day, celebrated on the last Monday in May, and instead celebrated Confederate Memorial Day, which is absurdly still an official state holiday in Alabama, Mississippi, and South Carolina. Here I mark one of the few benefits of segregated schools, where I spent my pre-high school years: black principals ignored Confederate Memorial Day.

BY THE 1990S, THOUGH, a few courageous white Southern leaders had begun to campaign against the iconography of the Lost Cause, especially the Rebel flag, which was raised above government buildings in a number of Southern states, in large part as a defiant response to the 1954 Supreme Court ruling in *Brown v. Board of Education* that segregated schools were unconstitutional. In 1993, Georgia Governor Zell Miller issued a powerful call to remove the Rebel emblem from his state's official flag, to which the Southern Cross had been added in 1956. In Alabama, the Rebel flag was placed atop the state capitol in 1963 during the first George Wallace administration, where it stayed despite successive lawsuits by a persistent black state representative across three decades; finally Governor Jim Folsom Jr. let the Rebel flag come down in 1993.

The change Governor Miller backed in Georgia didn't immediately succeed, but his successor Roy Barnes managed to get a Rebel-free compromise flag raised in 2001, and the present state flag, without any Confederate symbology, was approved by state voters and raised in 2004.

Miller had laid out the issues a decade earlier. A native of the North Georgia mountains who spoke with a deep Southern twang, he could hardly have been mistaken for an outsider who simply didn't understand. His ancestors had fought for the Confederacy. He would go on to serve in the U.S. Senate as an irascible and unpredictable Democratic centrist. In his speech on the flag, he said, in part:

> Of all the arguments that have been made for keeping this flag, the most infuriating to me is the contention that if we don't we will somehow forget the sacrifices made by those who fought for the Confederacy. We will not forget. We cannot forget. Our graveyards, our literature and many of our own family histories will forever keep alive the memory of those who died for the Confederacy—and the memory of those whose freedom from slavery depended on the Confederacy's defeat . . .
>
> But I also cannot forget the millions of Georgians, my ancestors and yours, who also made sacrifices in other wars, both before and after the War Between the States. And in reverence to their memory, I cannot accept the idea that the brief, violent and tragic period of the Confederacy is the only part—the only part—of our long history that defines our identity . . .
>
> For four brief years—that's 1.5 percent of our state's entire history—Georgia was a member of the Confederate States of America. Yet it is the Confederacy's most inflammatory symbol that dominates our [state] flag today. We all know why. And it has nothing to do with the bravery of the Confederate troops . . . . It is clear the [state] flag was changed in 1956 to identify Georgia with the dark side of the Confederacy—both the desire to deprive some Americans of the equal rights that are the

birthright of all Americans, and yes, the determination to destroy the United States if necessary to achieve that goal.

Miller was no fool. He was a shrewd politician who'd already counted votes in the Georgia General Assembly, and he knew he would lose on the flag issue, despite having delivered the speech of his career.

I, TOO, KNEW HE'D lose. As editorial page editor of the *Atlanta Constitution*, I, too, had crusaded against the Rebel flag as an official state symbol, writing opinion pieces, giving speeches, participating in panel discussions. I challenged the notion of "happy slaves," "good slave owners," and the Rebel flag as a necessary symbol of heritage. I was told that I didn't understand the South, though I'm as Southern as gravy on biscuits. I was told that I didn't understand "heritage," though I understood the difference between theirs and mine quite well. I was told that I wanted to rewrite the past, though I wasn't the revisionist in the room. I am still stunned by the level of self-deception among Confederate sympathizers and taken aback by the mind-torturing contradictions required for them to believe Lost Cause lies.

One hardy alternative fact that Lost Cause adherents frequently hold up as "evidence" of enslaved men's happy lot was the claim that many slaves had fought for the Confederacy. I usually laughed out loud when I heard that one and challenged the speaker to show a picture of a black man in a Confederate uniform holding a rifle. Not a single reputable historian of the Civil War claims that any black men were Confederate soldiers. Indeed, the Confederacy banned black men from military service.

There were plenty of enslaved men in Confederate camps, of course, since their owners often took them along to take care of horses, set up camp, work as blacksmiths, cook, clean and even tend the wounded.

But give them weapons? There may have been occasions when an enslaved man picked up a musket a soldier had dropped and fired it toward Union troops as they were closing in. Some stayed and loyally served their owners even when they had the chance to escape. Far, far more black men took the opportunity of the chaos of war to run to freedom behind Union lines.

As the war dragged on, a few Confederate officers did push to dragoon the enslaved or pay freed black men for military service, but they were rebuffed. Writing about the Lost Cause mythology in the *Atlantic*, Clint Smith quoted Confederate General Howell Cobb: "If slaves will make good soldiers, our whole theory of slavery is wrong."

Though Zell Miller's 1993 speech did not inspire an immediate reckoning with revisionist Civil War history, most Southern states and large cities had activists and political leaders who kept pushing toward progress, who kept insisting on revamping state flags and moving monuments and renaming streets that had honored Confederates and Klansmen. The Charleston massacre in 2015 added momentum. Places that had dithered and ducked and dodged now got about the business of moving Confederate generals from their pedestals in public spaces. So it was that the Charlottesville, Virginia, city council voted in February 2017 to remove a statue of Robert E. Lee, astride his steed, from a public park named for him.

Not all Southerners were happy about abandoning the myths

they had learned as children. The wave of historical corrections was another huge adjustment in an era of mind-boggling cultural change. If they lost the past, those white Southerners feared, wouldn't they lose the future, too? Indeed, a visceral fear of losing the future to demographic decline—a fear widespread not only among white Southerners but among white Americans more broadly—animated the campaign of Donald J. Trump and powered his path to the presidency.

But few whites, not even the adherents to the Lost Cause, want to be associated with the word "racism." As Charlottesville worked toward moving Lee's statue, his sympathizers mostly expressed their anger through tirades at public meetings and threatening phone calls to local leaders. They argued that their protests were justified to protect (white) Southern heritage. They wanted nothing to do with overt gestures of white extremism.

Of course, there were exceptions like Jason Kessler, a Charlottesville native and 2009 graduate of the University of Virginia. An odd character with a checkered history, Kessler had once manned phones for a Democratic polling service and had, according to friends, voted for President Barack Obama. He had spent time in Charlottesville's Occupy Wall Street encampment.

But Kessler, who had trouble holding down a job, was an angry young man in search of a cause. White supremacist groups attract many such young white men, and by the time Trump started his presidential campaign in earnest, Kessler was gravitating toward the far-right. Trump, after all, seemed an ally.

Looking for stature among his new crowd, Kessler found an enemy in Wes Bellamy, a black teacher serving as vice mayor of Charlottesville. In March 2016, Bellamy had held a news conference calling for the removal of the Lee statue. At a council meeting later that year, Kessler marched to the front of the gathering and denounced Bellamy as a "black supremacist." He had found his cause.

Having met white nationalist Richard Spencer and some of the other leaders of the "alt-right"—a clever euphemism for the new racists—Kessler by now had a stage to organize a "Unite the Right" rally in Charlottesville.

Unite the haters, it did.

On Friday, August 11, 2017, an assortment of bigots began gathering at the park—white supremacists, neo-Nazis, Confederate sympathizers, Klansmen—to protest removal of the Lee statue. They were met by counter-protestors. By Saturday morning, approximately five hundred racists were met by about one thousand counter-protestors, with people on both sides shouting and shoving. By noon, Virginia Governor Terry McAuliffe declared a state of emergency and the Virginia State Police pronounced the rally an unlawful assembly. Riot police cleared the park.

As police pushed the crowd out of the park, protestors and counter-protestors were squeezed together and exchanged insults. One right-wing protestor speared counter-protestor Corey Long with a flagpole; twenty-year-old DeAndre Harris, a fellow counter-protestor, tried to intervene. Harris was set upon by a group of bigots and severely beaten.

At around 2 p.m. that afternoon, white supremacist James Alex Fields Jr. deliberately rammed his car into a crowd of counter-protestors, injuring nineteen people and killing thirty-two-year-old Heather Heyer. Even then-U.S. Attorney General Jeff Sessions, an Alabamian with no sympathy for civil rights causes, described the episode as domestic terrorism. But President Trump could not bring himself to utter those words. He had long used hateful rhetoric to signal his sympathy for the views of white nationalists and their allies.

Still, it was jarring to hear him address the Charlottesville rampage by launching into a pattern of false equivalence. On the Saturday evening after Heyer and others were mowed down, Trump condemned "this egregious display of hatred, bigotry and violence on many sides, on many sides." A few days later, in response to reporters' questions, he waded further into a morass of equivocation and sophistry, suggesting that the movement to replace Confederate markers was misguided. Asked if the attack on Heyer should be categorized as terrorism, Trump said:

> You can call it terrorism. You can call it murder. You can call it whatever you want. . . . That was a horrible day . . . I watched . . . much more closely than you people watched it . . . you had a group on one side that was bad, and you had a group on the other side that was also very violent. And nobody wants to say that, but I'll say it right now. . . . I think there's blame on both sides. And I have no doubt about it . . . you had some very bad people in [the neo-Nazis], but you also had people that were very fine people, on both sides. . . . You had people in that group . . . that were there to protest the taking down of, to them, a very, very important statue and the renaming of a park from Robert E. Lee to another name.

By then, even the conservative *National Review* had expressed disappointment in Trump's response, noting that he was reluctant to condemn the bigots who showed up in Charlottesville because they constituted part of his base. Its editors addressed the unfortunate alliance in an editorial:

> This is somewhat awkward for President Trump because the cracked and malevolent young men raging about "white genocide" are his people, whether he wants them or not. Let us be clear about what we mean by that: President Trump obviously has defects and shortcomings as a political leader, but we do not believe for a second that those failures include a sneaking anti-Semitism or a secret taste for neo-Confederate revanchism. At the same time, he has made common cause with those who have flirted with those elements for political and financial gain.

The depth of Trump's taste for antisemitism and "neo-Confederate revanchism" may have been debatable in 2017, but it is clear he wanted the bigots to stay in his camp. He courted them. Though several prominent Republicans issued strong denunciations of the extremists who gathered at Charlottesville, Trump did not. Weren't they merely carrying out his plans? As former KKK leader David Duke said about the Charlottesville gathering, the extremists would "fulfill the promises of Donald Trump" to "take our country back." And by then it was increasingly clear what the MAGA-hatted crowd wanted to "take our country back" to—to the 1950s and unquestioned white, Christian, male, heterosexual domination of culture, politics, and law.

The Trump family's history of racist practices in real estate transactions is a matter of public record, but Donald Trump's affection for the Lost Cause was nevertheless puzzling. Born and bred in Queens, New York City, he had no familial or cultural connections to the Old Confederacy and its Lost Cause iconography. Still, he insisted on becoming the neo-Confederates' most prominent champion. Trump chose to walk boldly backwards to a time when white supremacy was an accepted pillar of American culture.

A few years after Charlottesville, he sparred with his own Pentagon officials who wanted to retitle military bases that are named for Confederate leaders, including Georgia's Fort Benning (General Henry Benning), Texas's Fort Hood (General John Bell Hood), and North Carolina's Fort Bragg (General Braxton Bragg), to list just three of the ten major ones. Trump vetoed a pivotal defense spending bill because it included instructions to rename the bases, but a GOP-controlled Senate easily overrode the veto (though the renaming has not yet happened, was placed in the hands of a commission in 2021, and may happen by 2024).

IF NEWTON'S THIRD LAW of Motion applies to skirmishes over foundational truths, Trump's demagoguery may have sparked the largest protest movement since the 1960s. The Black Lives Matter movement was born in 2013 in the wake of the acquittal of George Zimmerman, who shot and killed Trayvon Martin, an unarmed black teenager who was walking home from a store in Sanford, Florida. BLM activism and national acceptance grew after the police killings of two unarmed black men in 2014—Michael Brown in Ferguson, Missouri, and Eric Garner in New York City. But its protests remained sporadic and largely localized.

That changed in 2020. Perhaps it was the cumulative effect of so much police violence. Perhaps it was the trauma of the COVID-19 pandemic, which especially slammed communities of color, killing old and young alike and stripping away jobs and paychecks. Or perhaps it was simply the courage of a black teenager, Darnella Frazier. On May 25, 2020, she videoed a Minneapolis police officer, Derek Chauvin, with his knee on the neck of George Floyd as he struggled to breathe.

Cellphone cameras had already changed the way much of the nation viewed police violence, in the same way that network television footage had changed the way many Americans saw the civil rights movement. It is hard to justify vicious law enforcement officers beating unarmed, peaceful civil rights protestors. And it is hard to justify vicious law enforcement officers beating, choking, or shooting unarmed, already subdued black men.

While Chauvin kept his knee on Floyd's neck for more than nine minutes, Frazier's video started as Floyd was struggling to breathe, gasping for air, begging to be let go. "Please, please, please," he said. "I can't breathe," he said more than twenty times. "Mama," he called out, shortly before he went quiet and said no more and breathed no more.

Frazier kept her cellphone camera aimed at the police officers even while they menaced bystanders. Her video not only led to charges against Chauvin but also ignited a global movement of protests against police violence. And because of Frazier's courage, Chauvin was convicted of second- and third-degree murder—a rare case of justice for a brutal police officer—and sentenced to two decades in prison. In June 2021, the board that administers the Pulitzer Prize, the most prestigious honor in journalism, gave

Frazier, even though she was not a news reporter, a special citation for "courageously reporting the murder of George Floyd, a video that spurred protests against police brutality around the world, highlighting the crucial role of citizens in journalists' quest for truth and justice."

Though there was no video capturing the 2020 fatal shooting of twenty-six-year-old Breonna Taylor, her case drew worldwide attention in the wake of Floyd's death. Taylor, an emergency room technician with no criminal record, was shot dead in her own home by Louisville, Kentucky, police officers executing a no-knock warrant. Her boyfriend, Kenneth Walker, thought the police were intruders breaking in and fired toward the apartment's door. Police returned a barrage of gunfire, hitting Taylor six times. Nothing illegal was subsequently found in her apartment.

The Black Lives Matter movement also brought widespread attention to the 2020 fatal shooting of twenty-five-year-old Ahmaud Arbery, killed not by police officers but by civilians with close connections to police and prosecutors in southeast Georgia. Arbery, who had been a high school football standout, was jogging on a sunny Sunday afternoon in a predominantly white suburban community near Brunswick. He stopped and looked around inside a house under construction and then resumed his jog.

He was confronted by two armed white men, former Glynn County police officer Gregory McMichael, and his son, Travis, who followed Arbery in a pickup truck. They ordered Arbery to stop, but he tried to get around their vehicle. They blocked him, and the younger McMichael got out of the truck. Struggling with Travis, Arbery was shot dead at point-blank range.

For more than two months, the McMichaels were not charged with any crime. They claimed they were attempting a citizen's arrest of a suspect they believed had burglarized homes in their neighborhood. Before recusing himself from the case because of his professional connection to the elder McMichael, the local prosecutor recommended that no charges be filed against the father and son. In his view, they had acted in self-defense.

Local whites in the criminal justice system were so certain of the McMichaels' righteousness, so secure in their white privilege, that a family friend, an attorney, released a cellphone video of the entire episode that had been taken by a third man, William Bryan, a neighbor of the McMichaels who had followed the pursuit in his vehicle. The video of Arbery being set upon by the McMichaels quickly spurred outrage, and all three men, Bryan included, were arrested and charged.

BLACK LIVES MATTER PROTESTS lasted through the summer of 2020. White, black, and brown people gathered in Minneapolis, Atlanta, Chicago, New York, Louisville, and Portland. They gathered in small towns and rural communities, from 4S Ranch, California, to Woburn, Massachusetts, from Taylorville, Illinois, to Aledo, Texas. They gathered in London, Nairobi, Kyoto, Warsaw, Stockholm, Paris, Buenos Aires, and Bogota. Protests took place in more than sixty cities on all seven continents.

While the demonstrations were overwhelmingly peaceful, some were accompanied by sporadic violence (often when white supremacist counter-protestors got involved). Trump tried to use those incidents not only to smear the entire BLM protest movement but also to gin up fear among the white voters he needed to salvage his reelection campaign that was faltering in part because of his disastrous response to the COVID-19 pandemic.

The president's most dramatic attempt to portray himself as the white savior of besieged white citizens backfired spectacularly. On June 1, 2020, as a peaceful crowd of thousands of BLM protestors gathered across from the White House, Trump decided to project an image of strength by removing the protestors by the forceful use of several federal law enforcement agencies and National Guard troops. Snipers were stationed on rooftops as helicopters circled overhead. Police and soldiers released tear gas and flash-bang grenades on the stunned crowd. Protestors were left choking, coughing, and running.

As the chaos cleared, Trump—never a churchgoer—walked triumphantly across Lafayette Square to St. John's Episcopal Church, accompanied by several officials, including combat fatigues-wearing General Mark Milley, then the chairman of the Joint Chiefs of Staff. When Trump arrived in front of the church, he held up a Bible handed to him by his daughter for what he believed would be the perfect photo-op.

But images of troops shoving, clubbing, and chasing peaceful demonstrators drew outrage not only from Democrats but from a few Republicans, who noted that the misbegotten affair resembled a scene from a banana republic. Representing a military culture that is emphatic about its duty to remain outside partisan politics, Milley later apologized for his involvement in the spectacle.

Trump, however, was undeterred. In his search for cultural scapegoats, he soon picked Bubba Wallace, the only African American driver competing at the highest level of NASCAR.

On June 10, 2020, in a race at Martinsville, Virginia, Wallace, a native of Mobile, Alabama, drove a car with a Black Lives Matter decal on the rear quarter panel, and a black hand clasping a white one on the hood. He also pushed NASCAR to prohibit the display of Confederate flags at its races—a long-time tradition among the mostly white crowds who populated the infields at historic racetracks like those in Darlington, South Carolina, or Talladega, Alabama.

When NASCAR agreed to the flag ban, beginning in July at Talladega, Wallace and his team were treated to a chilling sight. The pull rope on their garage stall at the Talladega track had been fashioned into a hangman's noose. Notwithstanding the racial implications, the FBI concluded that the noose had been there before the stall was assigned to Wallace, thus he was not targeted and no hate crime had been committed. President Trump rushed into the fray. In a tweet, he demanded to know:

> Has @BubbaWallace apologized to all of those great NAS-CAR drivers & officials who came to his aid, stood by his side, & were willing to sacrifice everything for him, only to find out that the whole things was just another HOAX?

Racist fans howled in agreement. The son of one former driver declared on Facebook, "I wish they would've tied [the noose] to him and drug him around the pits." But team owner Richard Petty, one of the most venerated figures in stock car racing, stood by his driver. "There is absolutely no place in our sport or society for racism," he declared. "I stand shoulder to shoulder with Bubba yesterday, today, tomorrow, and every day forward."

ALL OF THIS WAS emblematic of the national mood—divided, often bitter—as President Trump, with deepening desperation, pursued reelection. His effort was crippled by the staggering death toll from COVID-19, as well as the pandemic's ruinous effect on the economy. As Trump frantically tried to shake off responsibility for infections in the United States, he pointed the finger at China, using racially tinged rhetoric: "China virus," "Wuhan virus," "Kung flu."

His demagoguery didn't curb the death toll. It merely emboldened racists and excused ignorance, putting Asian Americans at risk. The elderly were accosted and beaten on street corners. Doctors and nurses were threatened. Children were bullied at school.

In the end, the combination of Trump's bigotry, mendacity, and sheer incompetence upended a campaign he had expected to be a cakewalk to victory. Voters were soothed by a calm and steady Joe Biden, who promised to restore normalcy.

Biden's Road to Georgia

Cynthia Tucker

By 2020, Joseph Robinette Biden had run for the presidency twice but had never won a Democratic primary. Not one.

When he began his first campaign, for the 1988 Democratic nomination, he was considered presidential timber, having served in high-profile roles in the Senate. But back then presidential contenders were expected to exhibit a finely honed sense of ethics—at least in the public sphere—and Biden was accused of plagiarizing a speech. He received so much negative news coverage that he dropped out.

Biden next sought the Democratic nomination in 2008, running as the seasoned veteran who would bring decades of experience to the job. He was quickly out-paced by another seasoned player, Senator Hillary Clinton, and a young upstart, Senator Barack Obama. Obama became the Democratic nominee and chose Biden as his running mate. Biden's eight-year tenure as Obama's vice president was widely expected to be the capstone of his career.

Biden and Obama forged a genuine friendship, but Obama was said to be less than enthusiastic when Biden considered running for the 2016 nomination. Clinton had served ably as Obama's Secretary of State, and she was believed to be the superior candidate. Biden was by then in his seventies, a voluble elder statesman with a well-known habit of speaking off-key. He had referred to himself as a "gaffe machine."

Moreover, Biden had been struck again by tragedy. He lost his first wife and their infant daughter in a car wreck in 1972. Grief washed over him, but he and his surviving two sons picked themselves up. Then in 2015, the elder son, Beau, died of brain cancer, and Biden was consumed by grief anew and said he wouldn't have been able to mount an effective campaign. He told CBS' "60 Minutes" that ". . . You can't run for president unless you throw your entire being into it."

Clinton lost to Trump in 2016, of course, and over the months and years to come, the Trump presidency grated on Biden. He decided to seek the presidency a third time, he said, out of a sense of duty. He wanted to protect the Obama-Biden legacy, which Trump had conscientiously set out to destroy and belittle, and he wanted to protect democracy, which he believed was under siege.

By the time Biden announced his candidacy for the Democratic nomination in April 2019, he was seventy-six. He would end up competing against a raft of Democrats, fresher faces such as those of Senator Kamala Harris and Mayor Pete Buttigieg, and not-so-fresh faces, such as those of Senator Elizabeth Warren and Senator Bernie Sanders, who is even older than Biden. In the 2020 campaign, Biden's poll numbers were usually higher than those of any Democratic rival, but his campaign struggled during the COVID-19 lockdown, and he was largely confined to virtual appearances from his Delaware basement.

Biden also failed to generate the excitement among younger Democratic voters that Sanders did. In the left-most precincts of the Democratic Party, it was taken as gospel that young voters would assure victory. And Sanders was on a roll, narrowly losing the first round of Democratic voting, the Iowa caucuses, to Buttigieg (Biden finished fourth), winning the second round, the New Hampshire primary (Biden came in fifth), and winning the third round, the Nevada caucuses (Biden came in a distant second). Out of money, Biden seemed finished. Political prognosticators began predicting that Sanders would become the Democratic nominee.

But the possibility of a Sanders nomination wasn't comforting to some leading Democrats, who believed that his policies could too easily be caricatured as radical. Though few would say so publicly, Democratic elders feared alienating the moderates—especially white moderates—who could be peeled away from Trump by a more centrist nominee.

Trump himself had long suspected that Biden would be his strongest opponent. It's no coincidence that Trump was willing to attempt to bribe the president of Ukraine—the issue that led to his first impeachment—for damaging information about Biden and his second son, Hunter.

Black voters, too, sensed that Biden would be Trump's strongest rival. Sanders's campaign had never caught fire among voters of color, anyway, especially the older black voters who are at the core of the Democratic base. Those voters knew Biden as the loyal lieutenant to the nation's first black president, and they returned the loyalty.

They also knew their fellow white citizens well, having had to learn their political habits and inclinations out of an instinct for self-preservation. Many whites who believe themselves to be free of racial prejudices nevertheless were stirred by Trump's siren song, which played to their implicit and unspoken fears of black crime and loss of status. Among my mother's generation of black voters and among mine, few believed that Sanders, with his constant harangues demonizing the status quo, could defeat Trump. Given that ousting Trump was a matter of some urgency for those voting blocs, they supported Biden with enthusiasm.

With Trump's defeat a priority, South Carolina's black powerbroker, U.S. Representative James Clyburn, endorsed Biden three days before the South Carolina primary. Clyburn is a wily pragmatist, and he too was worried that Trump would effortlessly paint Sanders as a "socialist."

Now House Majority Whip for the second time, he is the most powerful Democrat in his home state, holding enormous sway, especially among black voters. After Clyburn's endorsement, Biden won the South Carolina primary with ease, walloping Sanders and leaving the others in the dust. That victory powered Biden into Super Tuesday, when fifteen jurisdictions held Democratic primaries. Though vastly outspent by Sanders, Biden did especially well among black voters, which set up the contest as a two-man race.

Clyburn is credited with rescuing Biden's campaign, and he deserves the credit. So do the rest of the South's black voters. In salvaging Biden's floundering effort, they gave the nation a nominee who could oust Trump. With that, black voters saved the world's greatest democratic experiment from a downward spiral into nationalist autocracy.

Of course, it was black Southerners who forced the United States to become a real democracy just a few decades ago. For all its bluster and all its myths, the U.S. was not a democratic nation until the Voting Rights Act was passed in 1965. Before that, many jurisdictions, most of them in the South, blocked citizens of color from voting. Because of the blood and tears and sweat and sacrifice of countless Americans—black, white and brown, some well-known and some lost to history—black Americans won the ballot during the civil rights movement, as did Latinos and Native Americans. That changed the nation.

Brave black Southerners had tried valiantly for full participation in the democratic processes at the end of the Civil War, with the passage of the Fourteenth and Fifteenth amendments to the U.S. Constitution. While women still did not have suffrage, black men organized, voted, and ran for office as Republicans. They were elected to local positions, to statewide offices, and to Congress.

But white Southerners were livid—despite the Nelson-Mandela-like forgiving attitude assumed by most black politicians. Whites complained, agitated and campaigned until President Rutherford B. Hayes withdrew the last Union troops from the South in 1877. Immediately, white Southerners began their campaign of terror, lynching, burning, looting, and generally menacing any blacks who dared claim full citizenship in the United States. It would be nearly another century before black men and women gathered the will and the resources to retake their rights.

South Carolina has a starring role in the story of the nation's halting march toward a more perfect union. The state was home to some of the earliest and largest plantations, vast fields planted with rice, cotton and indigo where men, women, and children of African descent were forced into lifetimes of unpaid labor, their children and their grandchildren handed the same fate. After the state became the first to secede in December 1860, young cadets from the Citadel Academy, manning a battery on Morris Island, fired on a Union ship in January 1861. Those were the first shots of the Civil War (three months before rebels fired on Fort Sumter).

After the war ended, South Carolina had the largest complement of freedmen in Congress, including the heroic Robert Smalls. At the outbreak of the war, Smalls had been assigned to steer the USS *Planter*, a small Confederate military transport, under the command of white officers. On the evening of May 12, 1862, the white officers left the transport for dinner, having given Smalls and other black crewmen permission to bring their families aboard for a visit. With the families on the vessel, Smalls steered the ship out to the Union Navy fleet in the Atlantic. That's how he and his crew escaped to freedom—a daring exploit that drew accolades throughout the ranks of Northern abolitionists and helped persuade President Abraham Lincoln to allow black men to enlist in the Union Army. Smalls later served as a pilot for the Union Navy. He returned to South Carolina after the war as a loyal Republican and was elected to Congress for several terms and served in the state legislature in between, fighting valiantly against the disenfranchisement efforts that had already begun.

As the twentieth-century freedom movement began, Clyburn, a student at South Carolina State College, joined it. As one of the "Orangeburg Seven," he helped to organize South Carolina's first student sit-ins. While in jail for his activism, he met the fellow activist who would become his wife, Emily England. Clyburn became an educator then a politician; his political career was, for him, simply a way to keep pressing toward civil rights.

With Atlanta as its capital city, Georgia had a special claim to civil rights activism. Atlanta was the birthplace of Dr. Martin Luther King Jr. and the city became the hub of the civil rights movement. King's undergraduate education was at the city's Morehouse College, the premier school for black men, and he followed his father to the pulpit of the city's Ebenezer Baptist Church; it was only natural that after he finished his pastorate in Montgomery, he made Atlanta the location for the organization he led, the Southern Christian Leadership Conference.

Atlanta offered advantages other than familiarity for the leaders of the young movement. It was home to a cluster of historically black colleges, most of which dated back to Reconstruction. As their graduates settled in the city, they created the foundation of a black middle class that would teach black schoolchildren, start businesses, open medical and law practices, and agitate for full equality.

Unlike Birmingham, Atlanta was also home to a handful of white business leaders with national ambitions, men who understood that their Northern peers would not negotiate deals in a city synonymous with church bombings and beatings of peaceful black protestors. It's not that Atlanta was free of racism and white resentment. It wasn't. But its business and political leaders, especially Mayor Ivan Allen, understood the value of putting on a proper public face. So it was that Allen and Robert Woodruff, the retired CEO of Coca-Cola and the dean of Atlanta's business community, pressured prominent whites to attend a dinner to honor King after he won the Nobel Peace Prize in 1964. How would it look to the world if they snubbed him?

After King's death, many of his lieutenants were still in Atlanta, working tirelessly to sustain momentum, even as the glory days of the movement seemed past. The Reverend Ralph David Abernathy, who co-founded the Southern Christian Leadership Conference with King, became its president after King's assassination and led the Poor People's Campaign to Washington later in 1968. The Reverend Joseph Lowery was there; he took over leadership of the SCLC in 1977. The Reverend C. T. Vivian had also settled in Atlanta, serving as chair of an organization that battled the Ku Klux Klan and other white extremists.

Just as Clyburn had, others saw political careers as natural extensions of the movement for equality. Andrew Young moved from the SCLC to Congress and was tapped by President Jimmy Carter to become the first black U.S. Ambassador to the United Nations. He was later elected mayor of Atlanta. Hosea Williams, who had marched across Selma's Edmund Pettus Bridge next to John Lewis, was elected to the Atlanta City Council.

Few did more to advance the cause than the late, great Lewis, who served briefly on the Atlanta City Council before seeking election to Atlanta's fifth Congressional district, from which he served for more than three decades. Lewis never lost his faith in the ballot as the great equalizer. As his remarkable life drew to a close, he penned an opinion essay to be published in the *New York Times* upon his death. He wrote:

> Ordinary people with extraordinary vision can redeem the soul of America by getting in what I call good trouble, necessary trouble. Voting and participating in the democratic process are

key. The vote is the most powerful nonviolent change agent you have in a democratic society. You must use it because it is not guaranteed. You can lose it.

Stacey Abrams was among the younger activists who heeded the call. She was born in Madison, Wisconsin, where her mother was studying to complete her master's degree in library science. Her parents then returned to their hometown of Gulfport, Mississippi, and that's where Abrams spent her early years. She has described her childhood as one of "genteel poverty," which meant "we had no money, but we watched PBS and read books." During Abrams's adolescence, she moved with her parents to Atlanta, where her mother and father pursued graduate degrees from Emory University and became United Methodist ministers.

She graduated from Atlanta's Spelman College, a storied HBCU for women, before earning a master's in public policy at the University of Texas and a law degree from Yale. Elected to the Georgia House of Representatives in 2006, she had begun her political activism long before that. She traces it to her childhood, when her parents told their children they were boycotting a local Shell gas station because of the parent company's business relationship to apartheid South Africa.

As a Spelman student, she challenged Mayor Maynard Jackson during a town hall meeting, asking him what he had done to assist impoverished young people. Recognizing a young star in the making, Jackson offered her a job in the city's office of youth services. After Yale, she worked as a tax attorney at a downtown law firm and later served as an Atlanta deputy city attorney.

While in the Georgia legislature—elected as House Minority

Leader in 2010—Abrams began to question the election strategy that moderate white Democrats had insisted for decades was the only way to win a statewide election: lure moderate white voters back to the Democratic Party. Abrams believed that many of those voters were likely lost forever (indeed, President Lyndon Johnson, after signing the Civil Rights Act in 1964, predicted that Democrats had just lost the South for a long time to come). Instead, Abrams believed, the party should pour its time and energy into bringing marginalized voters, especially voters of color, to the polls. Find the poor, she said. Find the oppressed. Find overwhelmed single mothers. Find disenchanted black men.

When the party's elders ignored her advice, she started an advocacy group in 2013, the New Georgia Project, which quickly took on the goal of registering those groups who had been overlooked by white Democratic operatives. Because of Georgia's long history of civil rights activism, there was already an ecosystem of voter advocacy groups, including the NAACP. The New Georgia Project brought a founder who was a shrewd fundraiser and strategist, elevating the work of finding and registering voters and getting them to the polls. In 2016, Abrams told *New York* magazine that finding and registering marginal voters required a serious financial commitment:

> That's not to say that there haven't been civil-rights organizations on the ground trying to tackle it, but it's expensive. You're not talking about a population that walks up to your door and asks to register; you're talking about a population that no one ever asks to register and therefore never thinks they should register.

Which means instead of standing at a festival (with registration documents), you have to go and knock on their doors.

And not everyone lives in Atlanta. Which means going to rural communities, going to depressed communities, going to communities where there is absolutely no trust in politicians. And that is an expensive endeavor.

Abrams employed that blueprint in her 2018 bid for governor, when she became the first black woman in the nation to be the gubernatorial nominee of either major party. She lost in a race marred by the voter suppression tactics employed by her Republican rival, Secretary of State Brian Kemp, who was in charge of the mechanics of voting. He used that power to disenfranchise hundreds of thousands who might have voted for a Democratic candidate. Still, Abrams lost by fewer than fifty-five thousand votes out of nearly four million cast. It was the closest race for governor in Georgia since 1966, when staunch segregationist Lester Maddox won.

Abrams made it clear that she didn't believe the election had been a fair contest, but she didn't sit on her hands and pout. She founded Fair Fight Action, another organization dedicated to voter outreach. By autumn 2020, a vigorous network of voter advocacy groups was working in Georgia to turn out a multiracial coalition, including Black Voters Matter, co-founded by Alabama native LaTosha Brown. The Georgia effort to get marginalized voters to the polls even included an online ad— "Get Your Booty to the Polls"—featuring nearly naked exotic dancers explaining that voters choose prosecutors, sheriffs, and school board members.

The far-reaching effort worked. Biden won Georgia, the first Democrat to win the presidential contest in the state since Bill Clinton's first run in 1992. Biden not only ousted Trump, but he also ushered in another historic ascension: the first woman vice president of the United States. Keeping a pledge to name a woman as his running mate, he had chosen California Senator Kamala Harris.

Harris is a woman of color and daughter of immigrants, the child of an Indian mother and a Jamaican father. Her parents brought to their new land a resolve to resist oppression, born of lessons from the colonialism that had scarred both their countries. When they came to the U.S., both joined its civil rights movement, participating in protests. That's how they met, and they taught their young daughters the importance of standing up for justice and equality. Harris was born to the march toward a more perfect union, standing on the shoulders of those who had started the journey in the Deep South.

Trump was so upset at losing his bid for a second term that he and his allies began a broad campaign to overturn the results, filing lawsuits and badgering GOP officials in states that he won in 2016. He insisted, falsely, that he had won, that the results had been skewed by massive fraud.

He was especially stunned by his loss in Georgia, which had been for decades a reliably red state, so he focused much of his wrath on Georgia's election processes. He badgered and berated the Republican officials who oversaw the election because they insisted that it had been free of fraud. Those officials included, ironically, Governor Brian Kemp, who had beaten Abrams by campaigning as a Trump apostle and employing every voter suppression tactic at his disposal. But he wasn't willing to wade into the fever swamps of the Big Lie.

Trump, a lame duck but still wielding the powers of the presidency, went so far as to call Brad Raffensperger, the Republican who had succeeded Kemp as secretary of state, to pressure him to change the vote count in the presidential election. Having learned of Trump's attempts to intimidate other GOP officials, Raffensperger had the foresight to record the phone call. The *Atlanta Journal-Constitution* and the *Washington Post* ended up with copies of the recording. Raffensperger insisted to Trump that the Georgia vote counting had been accurate, but Trump insisted:

> The people of Georgia are angry, the people of the country are angry. And there's nothing wrong with saying, you know, that you've recalculated . . . So look. All I want to do is this. I just want to find 11,780 votes, which is one more than we have. Because we won the state.

That was another lie.

Not only did Biden legitimately win Georgia, but a bigger upset was in the works. A convergence of circumstances had brought January 2021 elections to fill both of the state's U.S. Senate seats. One circumstance ties directly to Georgia's history of voter suppression: It is among ten states— seven of which are states of the Confederacy—that require candidates to win more than 50 percent of the ballots in the first round of voting or face a second round, a "runoff." Georgia implemented the rule in 1962, after its notorious county unit system, which boosted the influence of white rural voters over black urbanites, was struck down by the courts.

When first-term GOP Senator David Perdue faced Democrat Jon Ossoff in the November election, a Libertarian candidate, Shane Hazel, was also on the ballot and drew a smattering of votes. Neither Perdue nor Ossoff won the required 50 percent plus, so they would face off in a January second round.

The rules were different for GOP Senator Kelly Loeffler in her first election in November 2020. Loeffler had been appointed to the seat by Governor Kemp after Republican Senator Johnny Isakson retired because of failing health. Under Georgia's odd system, Loeffler would compete in a "jungle primary"—a special election in which anyone who paid the filing fee would be on the ballot—against twenty other candidates. She ended up with the second-highest vote tally, trailing Democrat Raphael Warnock, pastor of the historic Ebenezer Baptist Church. Since neither cleared the bar of 50 percent plus, they, too, would be in a January runoff.

Despite the opportunity for historic gains, runoffs made Georgia Democrats nervous. As Southern whites began to desert the Democratic party—a shift that was evident in presidential races decades before it was clear in state contests—Democrats started losing statewide runoffs. While voter advocacy organizations always devote time and money to get marginal voters to the polls for the main event, those groups are often spent by the second round. Additionally, runoffs provide less opportunity for voters to go to the polls early, and many black and brown voters find it difficult to get off work for a second round of balloting.

But Abrams and her allies knew that the stakes were high:

Control of the Senate—and Biden's agenda—would rest on the results of the Georgia runoffs. They kept working, and 228,000 voters cast ballots in the runoffs who hadn't voted in the November 3 election, according to an *Atlanta Journal-Constitution* analysis of voting records, which found that those new voters were a racially diverse group of younger adults—blocs that tend to support Democrats.

Democrats also got some unexpected help from Trump. The outgoing president was consumed with anger, obsessed with his loss, and determined to spread the lie that the election was stolen by voter fraud. When he went to Valdosta to rally his base in advance of the runoff, he buried his support for Loeffler and Perdue in an avalanche of falsehoods about a stolen election. As his supporters chanted "Stop the Steal!," Trump insisted: "They cheated and rigged our presidential election, but we'll still win."

His lies about a "rigged" system likely swayed more than 750,000 voters who cast ballots in the presidential election but didn't show up for the runoffs, most of whom were, according to the *Atlanta Journal-Constitution*, rural whites, who tend to support Republicans.

By the end of the evening of January 5, it was clear that Georgia would have its first black U.S. Senator. On January 6, as Trump supporters were storming the U.S. Capitol, news outlets declared Ossoff the winner of the other Senate seat. With that, Georgia had two Democratic Senators—Ossoff is the first Jewish Senator in the state's history—and the Democrats had control of the upper chamber.

It's worth noting that both men had important connections to the late John Lewis. The congressman had been a member of

Ebenezer Baptist Church, where Warnock had served as senior pastor since 2005. And as a sixteen-year-old, Ossoff wrote Lewis asking to become a volunteer in the congressman's office. They bonded, and Lewis became a mentor.

It's also worth noting that Warnock and Ossoff sometimes campaigned together, more frequently in the weeks leading to the runoff. One campaign T-shirt had the cutesy slogan: "Warnock your Ossoff." For those who remember the history of the civil rights movement, there was no surprise in their easy alliance. Jewish Americans were among King's closest advisers and supporters—and not just Jews from the Northeast. Atlanta's Temple—a prominent Reform synagogue on a tony stretch of Peachtree Street—was bombed by Klansmen in 1958 because of the outspoken support its rabbi, Jacob Rothschild, gave to the civil rights movement.

But those years have become muddled in memory and those alliances too easily forgotten. Warnock and Ossoff offered an updated version, a compelling symbol of the possibility of a new South rising: multiracial, religiously diverse, socially and culturally progressive.

Because he was elected to fill an unexpired term, Warnock must run for reelection in 2022. Abrams is said to be considering another run for the governorship of Georgia next year, too. Both campaigns will be challenging—demanding bottomless war chests, indefatigable effort by an army of volunteers, and no little bit of luck.

But moderate-to-progressive Democrats running in Georgia in the years to come will have the wind at their backs because of the state's changing demographics, which Abrams grasped before most political strategists did. As early as the 1970s, following the election of Maynard Jackson as Atlanta's first black mayor, metropolitan Atlanta became a destination for throngs of educated, middle-class blacks—some just out of college, others middle-aged workers fueling a reverse migration. As the metro area's black middle class grew in size and influence, its success fed on itself—drawing more and more black folk who wanted to be part of the magic of a city nicknamed "Hotlanta."

According to the *Atlanta Journal-Constitution*, the state of Georgia was 57.5 percent white in 2008 but only 53.6 percent white by 2020. As Jelani Cobb has noted in the *New Yorker*, the state's black population grew by 25 percent between 2000 and 2010, and the Latino population doubled to 9 per cent. By 2010, the Asian American population had grown to account for 3 percent. While much of that growth has been concentrated in metropolitan Atlanta, the state's smaller cities, including Savannah, Augusta, and Columbus, have also grown more diverse.

Georgia's Democratic-leaning coalition includes, of course, progressive whites, many of whom have moved South from blue states, drawn mostly by Georgia's churning economic engine. Atlanta's white business leaders of the 1960s would likely be stunned by the success of their campaign to paint the city as "too busy to hate," which made Atlanta an acceptable choice for Fortune 500 companies looking to plant a flag in the Deep South. Those corporations don't just bring jobs. They also bring a college-educated cadre of professionals who tend to be comfortable with diversity, who detest homophobia, who support reproductive rights and who believe climate change is a crisis. That doesn't bode well for Georgia's reactionary Republican Party.

The demographic changes forcing a political realignment in Georgia are evident in a few other states of the Old Confederacy, notably Virginia, North Carolina, and Texas. Virginia, whose capital city was the second and longest-serving capital of the Confederate States of America, long held pride of place in the mythology of the Lost Cause. Richmond boasted a prominent Monument Avenue, a tree-lined thoroughfare intersected by a mall that held massive statues and memorials commemorating Confederate leaders.

Not anymore. The campaign to move Confederate iconography from the boulevard picked up momentum in the wake of Dylann Roof's rampage and gained velocity after the murder of George Floyd. Most of the monuments have been removed. In a May 2021 essay in the *New York Times*, Richmond's young black mayor, Levar Stoney, described his decision to short-circuit the legal process—against the advice of city attorneys—to remove the statue of Stonewall Jackson in July 2020:

> On live television, we watched a hundred-ton crane lift Stonewall Jackson from his pedestal. Cheers erupted from hundreds who had gathered in the rain to witness its removal. Like other residents in our city that day, I cried. Over the next week, contractors removed fourteen pieces of Confederate iconography throughout the city.

Stoney's decision drew significant support but also death threats, he wrote. That has not stopped his city or his state from rapidly turning the page on an ignominious past. The twelve-ton statue of Robert E. Lee on horseback, which had looked down over the boulevard for more than a century, was finally removed in September 2021, after opposition was quashed by the courts.

As Virginia's northern suburbs have mushroomed into metropolitan Washington, D.C., the state has become reliably purple with a distinct bluish tinge. While its southern regions are still home to conservatives who tend to vote Republican, in 2021 Democrats controlled the governor's office and the Virginia General Assembly. George W. Bush, who carried Virginia in 2000 and 2004, was the last Republican to win the state's Electoral College votes.

North Carolina, though it does not match Virginia's history of prominence in the Confederacy, does share with every Southern state a centuries-long resolve to keep black people under the boot of whites. North Carolina joined the Confederacy late and even then some of its mountain regions rebelled, their residents preferring to stay with the Union. That ambivalence is brilliantly captured in the popular 1997 novel, *Cold Mountain*.

Still, just as soon as Union troops left the South, North Carolina entered a committed relationship with Jim Crow, passing laws to disenfranchise black citizens, setting up "separate but equal" institutions, and tolerating racial terrorism. The state's recent history includes the shameful tenure of staunch segregationist and homophobe Jesse Helms, who served as a Republican U.S. Senator for thirty years before finally retiring in 2003. His tenure was an homage to reactionary politics. He battled against reproductive rights, voting rights, and gay rights and filibustered against the bill making the birthday of Martin Luther King Jr. a national holiday. He blocked funding for the construction of a National Museum of African American History and Culture until his retirement, when the late Congressman John Lewis, who had doggedly pushed for a black history museum in the face of Helms's intransigence, could finally secure the support to get it built.

But North Carolina is also turning toward a more just future. Its current national figures include the Reverend Dr. William Barber, a powerful preacher and patient activist whose decades-long work has promoted him to icon status among social justice advocates. He organized the first "Moral Mondays," days of protest and civil disobedience meant to call attention to state and federal laws that perpetuate injustice. With his colleague at the Kairos Center of New York's Union Theological Seminary, the Reverend Liz Theoharis, he is attempting to revive King's boldest and most radical project: the Poor People's Campaign. It is an ingenious response to an era in which demagogues have employed racism and nativism to persuade struggling whites that struggling people of color are the source of their misery.

Barber told the *New Yorker*'s Jelani Cobb, "Poverty has been so racialized that most people don't even know that, in raw numbers, the majority of poor people are white." The "Poor People's Campaign: A National Call for Moral Revival" now has affiliates in more than forty states.

North Carolina has also benefited from the dynamism of three universities, the University of North Carolina in Chapel Hill, North Carolina State University in Raleigh, and Duke University in Durham. The three schools—all located in the Piedmont region—have gained such prominence in areas of scientific research that they have become known as the points of a "Research Triangle."

Drawn by the foundation laid by the universities' work, technology companies and related entrepreneurs have flocked to the region, bringing a professional workforce that is unlikely to indulge the future antics of a segregationist Jesse Helms or the delusions of a Donald Trump. No Democrat has won North Carolina's electoral college votes since President Obama's first election, but Trump didn't win the state easily in 2020. He defeated Biden by just 1.35 percent of the vote.

Perhaps no former state of the Old Confederacy has been more politically intriguing over the last couple of decades than Texas, the state so enshrouded in a mythology of frontier independence that it is sometimes still referred to as the Republic of Texas. While Democratic activists have hungered to push the state's politics to the left, voters have given Republicans the winning edge in most statewide races since the 1990s. Trump won the state in 2016 and 2020 with 52 percent of the vote. That narrow margin has only energized Democrats, who believe they can attract another 3 percent or so of voters. When Democratic Congressman Beto O'Rourke ran against GOP Senate incumbent Ted Cruz in 2018, Cruz won—but by less than 1 percent of the vote.

Still, the demographics in Texas are complex; they don't automatically give Democrats an edge.

It is easy enough—given Hollywood's version of history—to forget that the land that is now the state of Texas has long been ethnically diverse. Apaches, Comanches, and Kiowa, among other Native American groups, were there when Europeans arrived. Many of the aboriginal inhabitants of the area were rounded up, killed, or run off by European explorers and settlers.

Mexico claimed the territory until well into the nineteenth century, so there are Texans whose families go back for generations but who also have Mexican ancestry. But a peculiar feature of the treaty that ended the Mexican-American war gave those residents an unusual status. In *Politico*, Jack Herrera recounted the history of the Rio Grande Valley community, many of whose members call themselves Tejanos.

Mexico ceded the land north of the Rio Grande to the U.S., Herrera noted, but it insisted that former Mexican nationals be offered U.S. citizenship and be considered, for purposes of local laws and the U.S. Census, "white." That was crucial since Texas was a slave state. Tejanos were still subjected to segregation and many slights of the state's Jim Crow laws and customs, but their legal status as "white" provided them a buffer.

Political strategists, especially Democrats, were stunned by Trump's success with that group of voters, but they shouldn't have been. Many Tejanos are cultural conservatives who oppose abortion rights and own firearms. Additionally, they have enjoyed the privilege of being considered "white" on paper, which spared them the harshest edges of racist oppression. They would not automatically recoil from Trump's incendiary rhetoric.

That hardly means that Democrats can't win Texas. Though his margins were thinner than Hillary Clinton's, Biden still won the Latino vote statewide; he also won it nationally. Latinos will continue to lean left politically as long as the left supports their quest for full equality. So will Chinese Americans, Indian Americans, and Nigerian Americans. After all, the "rainbow coalition," as the Reverend Jesse Jackson aptly called it, exists because people of color have been denied the basic premise of their democracy: that all people are created equal.

Demography isn't destiny, of course. The Democratic Party has simply seized the opportunity it was handed in the 1960s, when President Lyndon B. Johnson supported significant civil rights legislation. As disaffected whites began to drift toward the Republican Party, the GOP began to pander to their prejudices and fears. That was a historic political reversal from the days of Abraham Lincoln, who associated his party with the movement for freedom.

In the coming years, the Republican Party might climb out of the fetid swamps of racism, misogyny, and homophobia and reclaim a conservatism that centers itself in fiscal restraint, limited government, and a strong national defense. Such a party could break apart the rainbow coalition and attract voters of color who share those values. But that perhaps-one-day GOP would not be in thrall to Donald Trump.

For now, however, the thrall continues, with Trump refusing to acknowledge that he lost reelection, and the refusal carrying dark consequences. Five months into the Biden presidency, Reuters reported ongoing death threats against election officials in multiple states. In December, armed protesters gathered at the home of Michigan Secretary of State Jocelyn Benson, and although she refused to discuss it, threats continued into the summer of 2021. Officials in Georgia were sufficiently frightened that they went into hiding.

They had good reason. This was Donald Trump's America, with violence a clear and present danger, and if the proximate cause was clear, the roots were complicated and deep, touching the marrow of American fear, touching the heart and soul of the South. Trump successfully resurrected the politics of George Wallace's long-shot 1968 campaign for the presidency—a campaign that rippled with bigotry and white grievance—because he detected a longing for just such a malevolent crusade in many white households across the land. A progressive New South, the South of attorney Bryan Stevenson and political activist Stacey Abrams and race-car driver Bubba Wallace, still offers inspiration to those who believe the nation can make good on its promise of equality for all. But the Old Dixie—its hallmark a shameful embrace of white supremacy—has found influence far beyond its historic borders.

God's Chosen

CYNTHIA TUCKER AND FRYE GAILLARD

Their messiah had called them forth, so they came. In the days after TV news outlets declared Joe Biden the winner of the 2020 presidential election, Donald J. Trump had told his apostles to come to Washington on January 6. That was the day, he told them, that the miracle for which they had been praying would come to pass—he would overturn a fraudulent election and his power would be restored.

What unfolded was not a miracle but a calamity. As Congress prepared to certify the election results—usually a pro forma proceeding—a frenzied mob stormed the U.S. Capitol, breaking windows, beating police officers, ransacking offices, stealing souvenirs, and threatening elected representatives, including Vice President Mike Pence, who had refused to go along with Trump's Big Lie. The images unfolding on television screens were shocking, bewildering, sickening. A man waving a Confederate battle flag was shown parading about inside the citadel of American democracy.

But the Rebel flag may not have been the most jarring banner waved that day. Among the surging throng of rioters were countless signs and flags carrying Christian themes: "Jesus Saves!" and "Say Yes to Jesus!" and "Jesus is my Savior. Trump is my President." One person among the crowd charging up the Capitol steps held a Bible aloft. As historian Peter Manseau wrote in the *Washington Post*: "The religious contexts and motives for the siege were not a fringe element. They were, for many involved, the underlying reason for the entire event."

Much about the Trump presidency was puzzling. But one of its most perplexing features was the unwavering loyalty—fanaticism, really—he elicited from conservative Christians. Trump could count on the support of that core constituency for all his policies and pronouncements, including his practice of encouraging violence against political rivals and the press, his policy of tearing babies from their mothers at the southern border, and his rhetoric that pandered to white supremacists.

Trump's formal courtship of the religious right opened with a speech at Liberty University in January 2016. The audience of some ten thousand listened politely as the presidential candidate spoke passionately about defending Christianity from its perceived political enemies. But students snickered as he attempted to quote from the New Testament, citing Paul's second epistle to the church at Corinth as "Two Corinthians" instead of "Second Corinthians."

If his long history as a self-indulgent libertine had not provided a clue, Trump's ignorance of basic Biblical fluency should have alerted conservative Christians to an obvious truth: he didn't take Christianity seriously. (Neither did Liberty's then-president, Jerry Falwell Jr., judging by later revelations.) Trump had no relationship with any church. Yet, the religious right swooned in adulation, as if Trump were Christ himself.

Shortly after that speech, Falwell gave Trump his full-throated endorsement. Falwell was one among a pantheon of conservative Christian leaders who enthusiastically backed the thrice-married adulterer who admitted to groping women, who paid a porn star hush money, who preached a gospel of hate toward people of color, whose business career was a long con, whose lying was prolific and habitual.

If the Reverend Dr. Martin Luther King Jr. had survived to old age, he probably would not have been surprised. He had seen through the preaching and politely worded prayers of conservative white ministers—especially Southerners—who wanted law and order but not equal rights, peace but not justice, calm but not change. King called them out in his famous April 1963 "Letter from Birmingham Jail" that addressed Birmingham clergymen who called his protests in that city "unwise and untimely":

> When I was suddenly catapulted into the leadership of the bus protest in Montgomery, Alabama, a few years ago, I felt we would be supported by the white church. I felt that the white ministers, priests and rabbis of the South would be among our strongest allies. Instead, some have been outright opponents, refusing to understand the freedom movement and misrepresenting its leaders; all too many others have been more cautious than courageous and have remained silent behind the anesthetizing security of stained glass windows . . .
>
> I have traveled the length and breadth of Alabama, Mississippi and all the other Southern states. On sweltering summer days and crisp autumn mornings I have looked at the South's beautiful churches with their lofty spires pointing heavenward. I have beheld the impressive outlines of her massive religious education buildings. Over and over I have found myself asking: "What kind of people worship here? Who is their God? . . ."

By the time he was jailed in Birmingham, King surely knew that many of the South's most vocal—and most violent—segregationists were members in good standing of Protestant churches, disproportionately Southern Baptist churches. The roster of committed racists included preachers, deacons, trustees, and Sunday School teachers. While less-affluent congregations were home to members of the Ku Klux Klan, more prominent churches were proud to include leaders of White Citizens' Councils—the KKK for the professional class.

In the nineteenth and early twentieth centuries, legalistic* Christianity, especially its fundamentalist and charismatic wings, found its warmest embrace in the South and in frontier regions —small towns and rural areas where formal education was truncated, expertise was judged skeptically and full-time preachers were hard to come by since they demanded full-time salaries. Those who flocked to legalistic Christianity, with its conservative beliefs and practices, welcomed a religion that taught them to rely on their own readings of the Bible, which they believed contained inerrant truth.

In that era, conservative Christians were also dubious about civic spaces, believing that God called them not to a ministry of

---

* In his perceptive and persuasive book, *Stealing Jesus: How Fundamentalism Betrays Christianity*, Bruce Bawer explores how the religious right warps the teachings of the New Testament. He describes "legalistic" Christians— fundamentalists, evangelicals, charismatics or some combination—as those who tend to read the Bible literally; who believe eternal life exists in a literal heaven; who believe only the "saved" will enter that heaven; who see Satan as a real creature; and who tend to distrust the intellect because it can be manipulated by Satan. They also tend to be exclusionary, defining those who they believe are Christians as those who adhere to the previously stated set of doctrines.

social justice that demanded political participation but rather to an individual salvation that emphasized sexual restraint. If they voted, they tended to vote for Democrats. The Republican Party, which served the interests of the wealthy and well-educated classes, was denominated by mainline Protestants, including Episcopalians, who were sometimes called "the ruling class at prayer." Remember that "in that era" refers to before the civil rights era, when the South was solidly Democratic and its elected officials were segregationist whites. After 1964, the parties began to flip as blacks, now able to vote, registered as Democrats and the segregationists fled to the GOP. For the past few decades, the South, with whites still in the population majority, has been solidly Republican.

OVER THE DECADES SINCE King's letter, the movement he led has sparked compelling—in many ways, astonishing—cultural change, leading up to the nation's current moment of racial reckoning. Legalistic Christians have changed, too. In the late twentieth century, they stepped raucously into the public square. These days, Southern Baptists count among their members powerful politicians, including Senate Minority Leader Mitch McConnell and former (and likely future) presidential candidate Senator Ted Cruz. Other legalistic churches count as members former vice president Mike Pence and Senator Tim Scott of South Carolina. The political, cultural, and theological views of the religious right are now embedded in the Party of Lincoln, who could not recognize it.

Still, the hedonistic Trump seemed a strange standard-bearer for churchgoing folk who profess to believe in personal restraint.

But they didn't just support him reluctantly. They embraced him. Televangelist Jim Bakker said God "anointed" Trump. Franklin Graham—rejecting the more inclusive and more courageous philosophy of his famous father, Billy Graham— said Trump would "go down in history as one of the greatest presidents." And Robert Jeffress, senior pastor of the thirteen thousand-member First Baptist Church of Dallas, defended Trump's support among ultra-conservative Christians this way: "Well, it's really not that hard to figure out when you realize he is the most pro-life, pro-religious liberty, pro-conservative judiciary [president] in history, and that includes either Bush or Ronald Reagan."

Reagan did not shy away from the noxious "Southern strategy" of pandering to alienated whites who were uncomfortable with the changes wrought by the civil rights movement. Reagan announced his 1980 presidential campaign with an endorsement of "states' rights"—code for support of segregation—in Philadelphia, Mississippi, infamous for civil rights murders that he didn't mention. His contemptuous descriptions of "welfare queens" made grifters of poor black women who needed public assistance.

Bush claimed to have abandoned the Southern strategy, but he uttered not a word of protest when his supporters started a whispering campaign insisting that his Republican rival, John McCain, had fathered a black child outside marriage. In fact, the McCains had adopted a brown-skinned Bangladeshi child, a loving act that Christians should have celebrated. Nor could Bush resist condemning affirmative action in college admissions, a practice that has only barely raised the numbers of black and brown college students at predominantly white universities but which has drawn vociferous condemnation from conservatives.

And, in keeping with conservative religious traditions, Bush and Reagan looked askance at homosexuality, opposed reproductive rights, and appointed only conservative jurists. Bush, indeed, was a self-professed born-again Christian and a member in good standing of the United Methodist Church. He spoke openly of the role of his religious faith in his successful battle against alcoholism.

So WHAT WAS IT about Trump that called forth hallelujahs from so many conservative white Christians, more than for his Republican predecessors? The history of Liberty University, the brainchild of Jerry Falwell Sr., illuminates the path that legalistic Christians trod to end in an embrace of Trump. It is a story that Falwell tried to erase.

Falwell gained national fame as a fiery opponent of abortion and equal rights for gays and lesbians, but his local community knew him as a staunch segregationist through the 1970s. From his pulpit at the Thomas Road Baptist Church in Lynchburg, Virginia, he denounced the civil rights movement and racial integration. *The Nation* reports that in a sermon from the late 1950s, Falwell attacked the Supreme Court's decision in *Brown v. Board*:

> If Chief Justice Warren and his associates had known God's word and had desired to do the Lord's will, I am quite confident that the 1954 decision would never have been made . . . The facilities should be separate. When God has drawn a line of

distinction, we should not attempt to cross the line. The true Negro does not want integration . . . He realizes his potential is far better among his own race.

Falwell went on to proclaim that integration will "destroy our race eventually," a fear that more recently has taken on the characteristics of an existential crisis among conservatives. With the election of President Barack Obama, they were awakened to the demographic changes that are rendering them less culturally dominant. When they insist that their religious liberties are being stolen away by secular elites, they are actually angry over the liberties finally granted to Americans who have been traditionally oppressed.

Especially black Americans. Pollster Robert P. Jones, a scholar and former Southern Baptist, explores the nexus connecting American Christianity and racism in his powerful polemic, *White Too Long: The Legacy of White Supremacy in American Christianity*. He explains that a traditional tenet undergirding conservative Christianity is the belief that:

> white supremacy is a divine mandate. Particular readings of the Bible provided the scaffolding for these arguments. Blacks, for example, were cast as the descendants of Cain, whom the book of Genesis describes as being physically marked by God after killing his brother, Abel, and then lying to God about the crime. In this narrative, the original black ancestor was a criminal, and modern-day dark-skinned people continue to bear the physical mark of this ancient transgression.

That interpretation requires a tortured reading of the Old Testament. Even if you take the Genesis story of creation literally, it states that Cain was physically marked so that he would not be killed—affording him a protection that was not offered to the enslaved. Further, Genesis states that Cain was exiled to the "land of Nod." Thus if it existed, it certainly was not in West Africa, from which the vast majority of kidnapped Africans were stolen.

Over the centuries, right-wing Christians have conflated the story of Cain with that of Ham, a son of Noah who was cursed by his father. Ham's descendants would become servants to the descendants of his brothers because of that curse, according to Genesis. (Through the mid-twentieth century, the Church of Latter-day Saints also used Ham's story to justify its bigotry against black members.) Ham's great-great-grandchildren, then, would have had to evolve as dark-skinned and kinky-haired to fit the right-wing narrative. Nevertheless, that is the Godly "distinction" to which Falwell referred.

In a 1964 sermon, Falwell smeared King as a communist subversive. After casting doubt on "the sincerity and intentions of some civil rights leaders such as Dr. Martin Luther King Jr., Mr. James Farmer and others, who are known to have left-wing associations," Falwell made his analysis of their intentions clear: "It is very obvious that the communists, as they do in all parts of the world, are taking advantage of a tense situation in our land, and are exploiting every incident to bring about violence and bloodshed."

Much of white Virginia was in agreement. James J. Kilpatrick, then the influential editor of the *Richmond News-Leader*, used his column to call for "massive resistance" to the Supreme

Court's edict desegregating schools. But the court order stood, and Virginia, like all Southern states, was forced to educate black and white children in the same public school classrooms.

Falwell's response was to start a private school, Liberty Christian Academy, which the *Lynchburg News* described in 1966 as a "private school for white students." Similar "seg academies" sprang up all over the South. Five years later, Falwell opened Liberty University, which would become a bulwark of right-wing religious ideology, sending its missionaries into powerful political and cultural institutions.

FALWELL COULD HAVE BEEN content with keeping out of politics—as he insisted that Dr. King should have. But a 1976 decision by the IRS changed the trajectory of Falwell's political activism and ultimately of the religious right. It was a decision centered around the nation's continuing failure to confront racism at its core.

In 1969, a group of black parents in Holmes County, Mississippi, sued the U.S. Treasury Department to prevent three local private academies from getting tax exemptions. As the parents pointed out, the schools were founded to further segregation. They should not have enjoyed tax exemptions as charitable institutions. When the parents secured a court injunction against the exemption in 1970, President Richard Nixon mandated a new policy: Discriminatory schools would not be eligible for tax-exempt status. Because Bob Jones University insisted that the Bible mandated segregation, its administrators refused to accede to the demands of a pluralistic democracy. After years of warnings, it lost its tax-exempt status in January 1976.

Falwell and his allies, including Bob Jones Jr., were livid. "In some states it's easier to open a massage parlor than a Christian school," Falwell inveighed. While Jones continued to insist that the Bible mandated segregation—his eponymous "Christian" university refused to admit black students—Falwell was savvy enough to understand that racism was a hard sell to a national audience. But the new IRS regulation—which required seg academies to answer questions about their admissions policies, among other things—had served as a powerful catalyst for legalistic white Christians: they were now ready to enter the political arena.

Roe v. Wade, the 1973 Supreme Court decision that legalized a woman's reproductive rights, was not yet on the radar as a core moral issue for conservative church-goers. When the decision was handed down, W. A. Criswell, a prominent Southern Baptist minister, praised it: "I have always felt that it was only after a child was born and had a life separate from its mother that it became an individual person, and it has always, therefore, seemed to me that what is best for the mother and for the future should be allowed."

But right-wing activist Paul Weyrich had been seeking an issue that would rally conservative Christians and push them into the public square. As he noted in 1990, he had tried out several issues, including pornography, prayer in schools, and, interestingly, the Equal Rights Amendment, according to *Politico*. He and Falwell eventually agreed that abortion could rally the troops and provide their movement a respectable moral covering. The Roman Catholic Church, after all, already had generations of doctrine that denounced abortion.

By the time Falwell co-founded the Moral Majority with

Weyrich in 1979, he had cleverly covered the tracks of his long-standing bigotry. He revised his resume as a committed Christian rallying to the unborn, a man of staunch religious principles who would protect the nation and "its pious majority" from a sinful secular elite.

Nearing the start of the new millennium, the Southern Baptist Convention decided that it too needed a makeover. The denomination was born of the same conflict that cleaved the fledgling republic in 1861. As northern Baptist churches began to count more and more abolitionists in their ranks, the Southern churches rebelled and formed their own denomination in 1845.

In the nineteenth century, pro-slavery ministers cited Bible verses to support white supremacy. They used not only a misreading of Cain and Ham, but also a command from the Apostle Paul, who preached subservience to the powerless in his letter to the church at Ephesus: "Slaves, obey your masters with fear and trembling, in singleness of heart, as you obey Christ." (Ephesians 6:5)

In 1844, the Reverend Richard Fuller, a prominent South Carolina theologian, was eager to dispute the abolitionist view that enslaving fellow human beings was immoral. He wrote a letter to a Boston newspaper, the *Christian Reflector*, defending "Domestic Slavery as a Scriptural Institution" by citing a passage from Leviticus 25:

> The Old Testament did sanction slavery. God said, "Both thy bondmen and thy bondmaids, which thou shalt have, shall be of the heathen that are round about you . . . And ye shall take them as an inheritance for your children.'"

It would take a century and half for Southern Baptists to formally renounce those views. In 1995, the delegates of the annual meeting of the Southern Baptist Convention finally issued a formal apology for the denomination's support of slavery and Jim Crow. The apology coincided with a period in which the church was courting black and brown members, many of whom share their white brethren's conservative beliefs on cultural issues such as homosexuality and abortion.

BY THE DAWN OF the twenty-first century, throughout the South there were multi-racial conservative churches—non-denominational mega-churches, especially—in which it seemed that Christians were beginning to live out a Gospel that teaches a profound brotherhood—and sisterhood—in Christ, a bond that transcends race and ethnicity. Not only larger cities such as Atlanta and Dallas but also smaller ones such as Mobile and Macon were home to diverse congregations of conservative Christians, mostly white but with growing numbers of black and brown members. Even as church attendance was declining nationwide, conservative churches seemed on the verge of sparking a renewal that might inspire a broader racial reconciliation.

Then came Trump. He tore down the fragile structures of racial reconciliation only recently under construction in legalistic white churches. And he exposed their old foundations of white Christian nationalism, loosely defined as the belief that the United States was founded as a Christian nation and that its laws should follow Biblical dictates. As legalistic white Christians read the Bible, its ancient texts command a rigid patriarchy, so churches and other important institutions are to be led by white heterosexual men. Trump pandered to these whites' sense of victimhood in a nation rapidly moving away from such beliefs. As they insisted their religious rights were being infringed upon, with a black man having been elected president and a U.S. Supreme Court blessing gay marriage, Trump vowed to protect them from persecution.

Four months before the 2020 election, Franklin Graham framed the possibility of Trump's loss in apocalyptic terms:

> I'm just asking that God would spare this country for another four years to give us a little bit more time to do the work before the storm hits. I believe the storm is coming. You're going to see Christians attacked; you're going to see churches close; you're going to see a real hatred expressed toward people of faith. That's coming.

Graham said that God had put Trump in the White House to defend "Western civilization as we have known it."

Trump lacked Bush's personal piety, but that didn't matter. Trump abandoned the racial code words that Bush and Reagan and their GOP predecessors had used, exchanging them for the explicit racist harangues of George Wallace. That didn't matter, either. It may have been part of the appeal.

It wasn't long before black and brown parishioners began to notice the adoration directed at Trump by their conservative white ministers and brethren. Some of those black members were already disappointed with the failure of their churches to address issues of racial injustice. Trump was a confirmation of their fears. An exodus started among congregants of color.

One of the most powerful voices of the disaffected belongs to Jemar Tisby, CEO of The Witness, a nonprofit collective he founded to educate and support black Christians. After undergraduate school at Notre Dame, Tisby obtained a degree in divinity from the Reformed Theological Seminary in preparation for ministry in the conservative Presbyterian Church in America. Early on, he was disappointed in his denomination's silence about racial injustice, especially police violence against unarmed black civilians. Still, he persevered, writing about systemic racism and societal injustice on a blog he started for The Witness (then called the Reformed African American Network).

A chasm Tisby could not cross opened over Trump, who infamously announced his first presidential campaign with ugly characterizations of Mexicans and Muslims. "It was a moment of stunning moral clarity for me," Tisby has said. "I thought, 'We have to denounce this.'"

Instead, exit polls later informed him that an overwhelming 81 percent of white evangelicals had voted for Trump. "It was such a betrayal because I had invested so much of myself into these communities. We had prayed together. They had held my son in their arms. I had waved the banner for this branch of Christianity. They didn't just fail a little bit; it was catastrophic, the failure," he said in a podcast.

Black members were not the only conservative Christians disturbed by Trump's hold on the faithful. Denison University political scientist Paul A. Djupe, who has studied the impact of politics on religious affiliation, told the *New Republic* that just over 20 percent of American evangelicals, or eight million people, left those churches between 2016 and 2020.

Beth Moore, one of the best-known evangelists in conservative Christian circles, is among those whites distressed by what she called "the demonic stronghold" of white supremacy on the religious right, as well as the "sexism and misogyny rampant in segments" of the Southern Baptist Convention. In 2021, she announced she was leaving the denomination. Her departure made headlines because she has spent decades as the popular author of Bible study guides and as a prominent lecturer, speaking in sold-out stadiums to women from all over the country.

She was never thrilled with Trump. She tweeted her disgust with him after the airing of the Hollywood Access tape, in which he boasted about groping women. But she too persevered, hoping she could encourage the denomination in which she had worshipped for so long to confront its sins. She had had her own brushes with the sexism—even misogyny—bubbling through Southern Baptist beliefs. In May 2018, she published an open letter to her "brothers in Christ" about the mistreatment she had encountered as a prominent woman in a church that demanded women step back:

> As a woman leader in the conservative Evangelical world, I learned early to show constant pronounced deference . . . to male leaders and, when placed in situations to serve alongside them, to do so apologetically . . . I wore flats instead of heels when I knew I'd be serving alongside a man of shorter stature so I wouldn't be taller than he. I've ridden elevators in hotels packed with fellow leaders who were serving at the same event and not been spoken to and, even more awkwardly, in the same vehicles where I was never acknowledged. I've been in team

meetings where I was either ignored or made fun of, the latter of which I was expected to understand was all in good fun . . .

About a year ago I had an opportunity to meet a theologian I'd long respected. I'd read virtually every book he'd written . . . The instant I met him, he looked me up and down, smiled approvingly and said, " You are better looking than _____."

He didn't leave it blank. He filled it in with the name of another woman Bible teacher.

But among conservative white Christians, Trump's campaign for reelection didn't bring deep reflection. They were his faithful, his fervent believers. By March 2021, Moore had had enough. As she told Religion News Service, "I don't identify with some of the things in our heritage that haven't remained in the past."

Days after Moore announced her departure, the misogyny she had decried burst into national view when Robert Aaron Long confessed to killing eight people at spas across metropolitan Atlanta, including six women of Asian heritage. He told police that he suffered from a "sex addiction" and was trying to remove the temptation presented by the spas, blaming women who worked at them for his so-called dependency. Long and his parents had been active members of Crabapple Baptist Church in Milton, Georgia; the congregation expelled him from membership after his confession.

THE RESIGNATION OF RUSSELL Moore (no relation to Beth Moore) served as another sharp rebuke to Southern Baptist leaders. In May 2021, Moore stepped down from his post as head of the Ethics & Religious Liberty Commission, the Southern Baptist

Convention's public-policy arm. A critic of Trump who pushed for racial reconciliation, Moore was already viewed skeptically by the hard-right members of the denomination. When his departure was announced, Wade Lentz, a Southern Baptist preacher in Arkansas, tweeted: "Russell Moore leaving the SBC is the best news I've heard since Biden has taken office! Go be a Democrat sympathizer somewhere else, Mr Moore."

If Moore is a "Democrat sympathizer," his views are curiously out of step with most liberal policies and proposals. His theology closely hews to that of the SBC's ultra-conservative interpretations of Biblical mandates. Not only an opponent of abortion and gay marriage, he also supports the denomination's insistence on "complementarianism" for women, which means they are to have different (read "lesser") roles, according to a 2016 profile in the *New Yorker*.

Still, Moore took seriously his duties as head of the arm of his church that highlighted ethics. He did not brook racism, lies, or misogyny. After his departure, letters were leaked that showed he had accused other Southern Baptist leaders of encouraging—or committing—just those sins. The *Washington Post* obtained a copy of a letter—written shortly after he had announced his resignation—to J. D. Greear, an ally who was then president of the Southern Baptist Convention, in which Moore outlined those charges.

> As I prepare to transition to my new role of ministry, I feel conscience-bound to put down in print for you what you and I have previously discussed—a matter that, in my opinion, is now a crisis for the Southern Baptist Convention. The crisis is

multi-pronged . . . as seen in the blatant, gutter-level racism that has been expressed to me behind closed doors along with the reprehensible treatment of my African American employees and our African American seminary professors by figures within the Southern Baptist ecosystem. In this letter, though, I refer especially to the crisis of sexual abuse as it related to the SBC Executive Committee.

Moore went on to outline several instances in which he (and Greear, apparently) were threatened with "censure" by members of the executive committee when they pushed for thorough investigations of church leaders accused of sexual abuse. He cited a "disastrous move" by a working group to quickly exonerate churches that faced "credible allegations of negligence and mistreatment of sexual abuse survivors."

The worst episode Moore outlined involved Jennifer Lyell (she has allowed her name to be revealed publicly). Formerly vice president at the Southern Baptist Convention's Lifeway Christian Resources, she was once the SBC's highest-paid female executive. She has reported that she was sexually abused by a former Southern Baptist seminary professor.

[Lyell] attempted to tell her story of abuse, through the channels of the Executive Committee, and her own words were altered by Executive Committee staff to make it seem as though this horrifying experience had been a consensual affair. I saw, first-hand, the sort of abuse this brought upon the survivor, not only on social media and through calls for her firing from her ministry position but even the word "whore" directed to her in a corridor at the Southern Baptist Convention. We saw the spiritual and psychic damage this did to her . . .

The tactics are as simple as they are ungodly. They wish to caricature media who report on sexual abuse as biased, sexual abuse victims as, at best, mentally disturbed and, at worst, as sexually-promiscuous sinners, and those who stand with those victims as 'liberals' or as dedicated to a 'godless and secular MeToo movement.' "

Moore noted, as he closed his letter, that he had been threatened and intimidated—subjected to countless "investigations" by his superiors—for standing with those victims.

In every one of these incidents, some of the people involved will say, "We don't want Dr. Moore (or J. D. Greear) to leave." And I believe they are telling the truth. They do not want us to leave because they do not want the constituencies to which we speak to leave. What they want is for us to remain silent and to live in psychological terror, to protect them by covering up what they do in darkness, while asking our constituencies to come in and to stay in the SBC.

The racism and misogyny that are bedrocks of right-wing Christian theology can hardly be blamed on Trump, whose rise to national prominence was merely convenient for a religious right unable or unwilling to recognize the full humanity of women and people of color, to coexist with legal rights granted to gays, lesbians, and transgender people, to make peace with modernity. Their Christianity is at war with religious pluralism, their white Christian nationalism in defiance of the U.S. Constitution.

King had asked, "What kind of people worship here? Who is their God?" Trump told them that their God was the right one.

BUT OTHER PROPHETS GAVE other answers. In the interplay of faith and politics, now such a powerful force in the country, there was also the image of Raphael Warnock giving his maiden speech in the U.S. Senate. Warnock was heir not only to the theology of Dr. King but to the very pulpit where King had once preached. On March 17, 2021, sounding much like a pastor, Warnock introduced himself to the Senate with a passionate affirmation of the right to vote:

> I am a proud son of the great state of Georgia, born and raised in Savannah . . . My roots go down deep, and they stretch wide . . . At the time of my birth, Georgia's two senators were Richard B. Russell and Herman E. Talmadge, both arch segregationists and unabashed adversaries of the civil rights movement. After the Supreme Court's landmark *Brown v. Board* ruling, outlawing school segregation, Talmadge warned that "blood will run in the streets of Atlanta." Senator Talmadge's father, Eugene Talmadge, former governor of our state, had famously declared, "The South loves the Negro—in his place. But his place is at the back door." When once asked how he and his supporters might keep black people from the polls, he picked up a scrap of paper and wrote a single word on it: "pistols."
>
> Yet there is something in the American covenant, in its charter documents and Jeffersonian ideals that bends toward freedom.

And led by a preacher and a patriot named King, Americans of all races stood up. History vindicated the movement that sought to bring us closer to our ideals, to lengthen and strengthen the cords of democracy. And I now hold the seat, the Senate seat, where Herman E. Talmadge sat. And that's why I love America . . . I believe that democracy is the political enactment of a spiritual idea: the sacred worth of all human beings.

All of this, he said, was the heart of the promise springing from his place. But there was another dimension to the story, an emerging threat to the foundations of democracy, spreading, like the progress he had seen in his life, from Georgia to every corner of the country:

> The people of Georgia sent their first African American senator—and first Jewish senator, my brother, Jon Ossoff—to these hallowed halls. But then what happened? Some politicians did not approve of the choice made by the majority of voters in a hard-fought election in which each side got the chance to make its case to the voters. And, rather than adjusting their agenda and changing their message, they are busy trying to change the rules. We are witnessing right now a massive and unabashed assault on voting rights and voter access unlike anything we have seen since the Jim Crow era. This is Jim Crow in new clothes . . . And the question before all of us at every moment is, what will we do?

This, he said, was the cold reality of our time.

Democracy in the Balance

CYNTHIA TUCKER AND FRYE GAILLARD

The Republican Party, the party of Abraham Lincoln, had once worn the mantle of emancipation, but the GOP abandoned its freedom song decades ago, opting instead for the discordant strains of white fear and grievance. Ronald Reagan gave the "Southern strategy" a warm smile, while Donald Trump seethed with contempt. Neither visage concealed the underlying message, which voters of color read as rejection.

As the nation grew browner, thoughtful Republicans began to see the limits of their decades-long reliance on stoking the resentment of disaffected whites. Trump's defeat in 2020 fit a pattern: The GOP's standard-bearer had lost the popular vote in seven of the last eight presidential elections.

After Barack Obama secured a second term in 2012, vanquishing Mitt Romney, GOP bigwigs launched a deep dive into their dismal record to figure out what they were doing wrong. Months later, they released a remarkably frank document called the "Growth and Opportunity Project"—an analysis, or "autopsy," as it came to be known, of the Republican Party's failures at the federal level, particularly the failure to win the Oval Office.

The findings may seem surprising now since they represent the antithesis of Trumpism, but at the time, the recommendations were simply a common sense wake-up call for a political

143

party that was dying of whiteness. The authors noted the demographic changes that were increasingly apparent throughout the country and urged party leaders to appeal to people of color, with specific recommendations for outreach to Latinos, Asian Americans, and black Americans. Noting the GOP's declining popularity among women and young adults, the authors also recommended proposals to win over more voters in those key demographic groups.

An overlooked section of the report encouraged Republicans to modernize their approach to the mechanics of voting. Since the start of the new millennium, the Republican Party had reinvigorated the old Jim Crow strategy of voter suppression, implementing strict voter ID laws that it insisted, implausibly, were necessary to prevent voter fraud. The GOP autopsy recommended instead that the party make peace with proposals to make voting more convenient. The report noted:

> In 2004, 76 percent of the electorate voted on Election Day; in 2012, 65 percent voted on Election Day, a decrease of 12 percent in eight years. The Democrats successfully front-loaded many of their votes this cycle, expanding their early vote and absentee reach and giving them a much better picture going into Election Day of who had already voted and who remained a target for their efforts. They continued to expand their advantage in early voting, and this cycle they ran a much more focused effort on absentee voting, which helped them close their margins.
>
> This trend in early, absentee, and online voting is here to stay. Republicans must alter their strategy and acknowledge the trend as future reality, utilizing new tactics to gain victory on

Election Day; it is imperative to note that this will be a critical cultural shift within the Party.

But something unexpected happened on the way to growth and opportunity: Donald Trump descended the golden escalator and took a torch to the report. Rather than court voters of color, Trump employed a campaign slogan, "Make America Great Again," that was code for "Make America White Again."

RATHER THAN EMBRACE SYSTEMS that encouraged every citizen to cast a vote, the Republican Party enthusiastically restored the old strategy of blocking the ballot, aiming squarely at those voters to whom the autopsy had recommended outreach: voters of color and young adults. The GOP's updated version of Jim Crow does not employ poll taxes or threats of violence, but it is no less anti-democratic in its goals, no less racist in its outcomes.

Trump did not invent the GOP's strange allegiance to the strategy of suppressing the vote rather than courting voters of color. As the civil rights movement was gaining ground, some enterprising conservatives had already decided on the anti-democratic path. During his Supreme Court nomination hearing, the late Justice William Rehnquist was accused of participating in a Republican "ballot security" project designed to intimidate black and brown voters in the early 1960s.

The twenty-first century resurrection of voter suppression may have begun in 2002, after Democrat Tim Johnson won a South Dakota race for the U.S. Senate by one of the narrowest margins in history—524 votes out of 334,438 ballots cast. Johnson was powered to victory after Democrats did a Stacey

Abrams on Native American reservations: setting up registration booths, hectoring voters to go the polls, ferrying them if they needed a ride. Johnson won the Native American vote.

Immediately, Republicans charged "massive" voter fraud; Rebecca Red Earth-Villeda, a member of the Flandreau Santee Sioux Tribe, was prosecuted for allegedly submitting fraudulent absentee ballots. Charges were later dropped after the prosecution's own handwriting expert concluded the signatures were not forged.

The facts hardly mattered to Republican strategists who were newly energized to suppress votes not only from Native Americans but also from other marginalized groups who might support Democrats. Soon enough, the American Legislative Exchange Council (ALEC), a right-wing organization that writes bills that are then introduced by Republican state legislators throughout the country, had authored strict voter ID bills that began popping up from South Dakota to Georgia.

The bills usually required a driver's license or other state-sponsored ID, a requirement aimed squarely at poorer voters of color, many of whom don't own vehicles. Because college students tend to lean left, some of the ALEC-modeled bills banned college IDs as valid for voting. In some states with substantial populations of Native Americans, voters were required to have a residential address, although many reservations have unnamed dirt roads, and many dwellings lack addresses.

Trump's Big Lie simply supercharged the GOP effort to block the ballot. Though some Republicans are so deeply enmeshed in the Trump cult that they still insist the 2020 election was stolen from him, the more sophisticated employ double-talk:

They insist that "ballot security" measures must be enhanced to instill confidence in a skeptical electorate.

In a March 2021 opinion essay opposing a new voting rights bill passed by House Democrats, former Vice President Mike Pence opened with several bits of misinformation. He wrote, "After an election marked by significant voting irregularities and numerous instances of officials setting aside state election law, I share the concerns of millions of Americans about the integrity of the 2020 election."

Republican election officials around the country, including Chris Krebs, who was in charge of election security for Trump's White House, have conceded that there were no "significant voting irregularities." Further, Pence failed to point out that the "concerns" of millions of Americans about election integrity were fueled by the lies of his former boss.

Nevertheless, even GOP officials who received death threats because they insisted that Biden won the election fairly became champions of new voter suppression laws. Georgia Governor Brian Kemp was among them—hardly surprising since he showed a facility for voter suppression in his own 2018 election. Georgia's new ninety-eight-page statute goes so far as to criminalize the practice of offering food and water to persons standing in long lines to vote. The champions of the new statute did not explain how that provision enhanced election security.

But the Georgia law goes much further than intimidation and inconvenience. It gives far-reaching power to the state legislature, currently dominated by Republicans, to interfere in elections, blowing up the guardrails that protected election integrity in 2020. It also strips away the traditional bipartisan composition of local election boards. County governing bodies, many dominated by Republicans, may remove election board members for aggressively pushing to make voting more convenient.

That already seems to be the case in Troup County, Georgia, where the GOP-dominated county commission removed a black Democrat, Lonnie Hollis, from the county election board shortly after the new law was passed, according to the *New York Times*. Hollis has advocated for Sunday voting and a new precinct location at a black church. "I speak out and I know the laws. The bottom line is they don't like people that have some type of intelligence and know what they're doing, because they know they can't influence them," she told the *Times*.

The Georgia statute also dramatically curbs the power of the secretary of state, who oversees the mechanics of elections, as a member of the state elections board; that official will no longer be a voting member. That's a transparent move to punish GOP Secretary of State Brad Raffensperger, who disputed the Big Lie. This revision also shifts power to the state legislature, which could attempt to change election results through its new influence with the state elections board.

OTHER GOP-LED STATES HAVE passed similar laws stripping power from secretaries of state, who oversee the mechanics of voting, and permitting the removal of county election officials for partisan gain. By September 2021, according to the Brennan Center for Justice, nineteen states had enacted thirty-three new laws restricting access to the ballot and handing power over elections to partisans. At this writing, more such laws were moving through legislatures around the country.

While the American Legislative Exchange Council led the suppression effort at the turn of the new century, the current wave of retrograde laws is spearheaded by Heritage Action for America, an affiliate of the powerful right-wing "think tank," the Heritage Foundation. *Mother Jones* magazine obtained leaked video footage of Jessica Anderson, executive director of Heritage Action, bragging to donors about the group's success: "In some cases, we actually draft (the bills) for them. Or we have a sentinel on our behalf give them the model legislation so it has that grass roots, from-the-bottom-up type of vibe."

She cited Iowa, among the first states to pass new voting restrictions. "Iowa is the first state that we got to work in, and we did it quickly and we did it quietly. We helped draft the bills. We made sure activists were calling the state legislators, getting support, showing up at their public hearings, giving testimony . . . little fanfare. Honestly, nobody even noticed. My team looked at each other and we're like, 'It can't be that easy,'" she said.

That's a breathtaking admission of a well-executed plan to dismantle a cornerstone of American democracy: the right to vote. The Grand Old Party has not only renounced the Growth and Opportunity Project but also cozied up to authoritarianism. If it cannot win elections legitimately, it will cheat.

But there is pushback. In March, within days of the passage of the Georgia laws, civil rights organizations including the NAACP Legal Defense Fund and the American Civil Liberties Union filed suit in federal court, alleging discriminatory intent. In June, they were joined by the U.S. Department of Justice, and Attorney General Merrick Garland suggested suits against other states might follow. In Congress, the House quickly passed two voting rights bills, which Republican senators promised to filibuster. When conservative Democrat Joe Manchin proposed a bipartisan compromise that included a provision for voter identification, Stacey Abrams and Raphael Warnock endorsed the idea. But in the Senate, there were no Republican takers.

SYNDICATED COLUMNIST LEONARD PITTS saw among Republicans—more broadly, among political conservatives—a common denominator of fear and loathing, a terror of the marketplace of ideas. "An opinion one can't defend," he wrote, "is an opinion not worth having. At some level, conservatives must know they fail that standard, so they work to undermine it instead, to make the world safe for ignorance."

As Exhibit A, Pitts chose Florida Governor Ron DeSantis, who supported both voter suppression and restrictive laws in the realm of education. In June 2021, DeSantis signed a bill requiring state universities and colleges to survey students and faculty on their ideological beliefs. Two weeks earlier, he had pushed to ban the teaching of "critical race theory," by which he seemed to mean something broader than the arcane 1995 book by that title. "Let me be clear," DeSantis said, "Teaching kids to hate their country and to hate each other is not worth one red cent of taxpayer money."

By late spring, five Republican-controlled legislatures, three of them in the South, had passed similar laws, aimed, it was clear, against teaching the hard history of race in America. Christopher Rufo, spokesman for the conservative think tank, the Manhattan Institute, explained that it was all a matter of branding. He boasted: "We have successfully frozen their brand—'critical race theory'—into the public conversation and are steadily driving up the negative perceptions. We will eventually turn it toxic . . ."

For Jelani Cobb, an African American staff writer at the *New Yorker*, this cynical strategy was a self-refuting cause for alarm. "Conservatives," he wrote, "are validating the very contentions that progressives have been making all along: that racism remains a vital force in American life, that it is deeply rooted in the American past, and that our politics have been shaped, with disastrous consequences, by efforts to utilize racism for political profit."

BUT THE STRATEGY WAS working. The chilling effect had already begun. In Oklahoma, where Governor Kevin Stitt signed a Republican bill into law, Oklahoma City Community College cancelled a class on race theory until administrators could evaluate both the class and the impact of the law. All of this happened just a few weeks before the one hundredth anniversary of the Tulsa Race Massacre of 1921, the most deadly of a series of violent attacks on black neighborhoods in American cities. The attacks began in the South, specifically in Wilmington, North Carolina, in 1898, when a mob of armed white men staged a coup—quite literally overthrew the racially mixed city government and installed a new one, even as they randomly attacked and killed black citizens.

In 1900 in New Orleans, violence raged for three days as police tried to arrest a black militant named Robert Charles, who believed in self-defense—armed and violent if necessary. Charles killed five police officers and wounded nineteen people before he was killed and his body mutilated by round after round of gunfire. White mobs roamed the streets, killing as many as a dozen African Americans at random. In 1906, similar bands of white vigilantes murdered black citizens in Atlanta after newspaper reports alleging an epidemic of rapes—none verified—by African American men. Two years later, the violence crossed the Mason-Dixon Line. In Springfield, Illinois, home of Abraham Lincoln before he was president, a mob of more than five thousand whites set off on a three-day killing spree after two black men were charged with rape and moved from the jail so they could not be lynched. Historians agree that the Springfield riot led to the founding of the NAACP.

In Chicago in 1919, a week of violent confrontations left at least fifteen whites and twenty-three African Americans dead and more than five hundred people wounded. A thousand black families lost their homes when they were torched by rioters.

Then came Tulsa. On May 31, 1921, rumors of an attempted rape by a young black man in an elevator prompted a killing spree that left as many as three hundred African Americans dead in a neighborhood known as Greenwood. The massive destruction wrought by the mob, some of it accomplished by explosives dropped from airplanes, left another ten thousand people homeless. Viola Fletcher was one of the survivors. A century later, at the age of a hundred and seven, she told her story to members of Congress. Her voice was strong and clear, her emotions measured and under control, as she remembered a night when she was seven.

On May 31 of '21, I went to bed in my family's home in Greenwood. The neighborhood I fell asleep in that night was rich, not just in terms of wealth, but in culture . . . and heritage. My family had a beautiful home. We had great neighbors. I had friends to play with. I felt safe. I had everything a child could need. I had a bright future. Within a few hours, all of that was gone.

The night of the massacre, I was awakened by my family. My parents and five siblings were there. I was told we had to leave and that was it. I will never forget the violence of the white mob when we left our home. I still see black men being shot, black bodies lying in the street. I still smell smoke and see fire. I still see black businesses being burned. I still hear airplanes flying overhead. I hear the screams.

In Tulsa itself, this history is preserved in Greenwood, a neighborhood once known as "Black Wall Street." Today, what you feel if you visit that place, with its outdoor murals, cultural center and museum, is not only the story of lunacy and rage— of racism turned savage and deadly. The heart of the history is black aspiration. Greenwood arose and prospered after the end of Reconstruction and during the early years of Jim Crow. There are multiple testimonies to go along with Viola Fletcher's about the hope and promise that went with living there. Amazingly, the neighborhood did not die after the massacre. In his documentary, *Blood on Black Wall Street*, which aired on MSNBC, correspondent Trymaine Lee recounts how Greenwood rose again from the ashes—quite literally—to become a stable, prosperous area, only to face new devastation fifty years later with Urban Renewal and a highway knifing through its heart.

"The ache of what happened a hundred years ago . . . is still being felt in the hearts of those in this community," said Lee.

"This community is desperately looking to be made whole."

As Governor Stitt signed the law banning the teaching of critical race theory, a ceremony accomplished in the shadow of the Tulsa anniversary, he seemed to be aware of the awkward timing. "We can and should teach this history," he said, "without labeling a young child as an 'oppressor' or requiring he or she feel guilt or shame." But what did that mean? Marisa Lati, education writer at the *Washington Post,* wrote about the new misgivings of public school teachers in the wake of Republican legislation: "In reality, there is no consensus on whether or how much critical race theory informs schools' heightened focus on race. Most teachers do not use the term 'critical race theory' with students, and they generally do not ask them to read the work of legal scholars who use that framework."

But that, in the end, may not be the point.

"Some teachers . . . worry that the legislation will have a chilling effect on robust conversations," Lati continued, "or could even put their jobs at risk . . ."

One person who understands the chilling effect—the broader impact of a broad set of laws—is journalist Nikole Hannah-Jones. "Laws are being passed," she told Chris Hayes on MSNBC, "to stop us from learning the truth about our history."

The chilling effect on classrooms is only the beginning. GOP politicians are weaponizing the issue of critical race theory for election campaigns. Republican Glenn Youngkin pledged to ban it from Virginia public schools, and he won the governor's office in November 2021. Similarly seizing on cultural issues, a black Republican woman, Winsome Sears, won the Virginia lieutenant governor's race.

Political pundits and Democratic strategists pointed to mistakes made by Youngkin's Democratic opponent, former Virginia governor Terry McAuliffe, and to President Joe Biden's sagging poll numbers, both of which likely contributed to McAuliffe's defeat. But Youngkin's victory is also a salient reminder of a longstanding truth: Even white "moderates" are fearful of losing their privileged status, easily conned into believing they are threatened by a fair accounting of the nation's history, vulnerable to the siren song of white grievance. Youngkin didn't just win right-wing Trumpists in rural parts of the state; he also won over many well-educated white suburbanites.

In 2019, Nikole Hannah-Jones became the target of that white anger over confronting the history of racism because she was the driving force behind the 1619 Project published by the *New York Times*. She won the 2020 Pulitzer Prize for commentary for the lead essay in the package of reporting that filled a special issue of the *New York Times Magazine*. Before conservatives had identified "critical race theory" as a rallying cry, they were denouncing the 1619 Project, a series of essays that drew attention to the four hundredth anniversary of the enslavement of black people on these shores. Before leaving office, Trump responded by appointing a collection of partisan hacks to a "1776 Commission" that would, he announced, write a report that would put a stop to a "radicalized view of American history."

Though Biden quickly terminated the commission and ignored its error-filled report, the attacks on Hannah-Jones continued. When her graduate alma mater, the Hussman School of Journalism and Media at the University of North Carolina, offered her an endowed chair, Walter Hussman, a wealthy Arkansas newspaper publisher and a benefactor to the school, lobbied the board of trustees against granting tenure to Hannah-Jones. He argued that her journalism didn't meet standards of "objectivity," though she won her Pulitzer for commentary, which has never been held to any such standard. Besides, the old news-gathering model of "objectivity" has long been used to hide a multitude of sins—from falsehoods that whipped up lynch mobs in the early twentieth century to a false equivalence that gave credence to Trump's lies in the early twenty-first.

If Hussman and his ilk are genuinely worried about truth and objectivity in media outlets that are supposedly disseminating news, they should be attacking the alarming influence of a hardy ecosystem of right-wing disinformation. Spreading lies about "critical race theory" and insisting that massive voter fraud kept Trump from a second term, reactionary talk radio hosts and cable TV pseudo-news shows have cultivated a cult-like devotion among their aging and overwhelmingly white audiences.

There have always been such propagandists among us, but they didn't always have such power. In the 1930s, a Roman Catholic priest, Father Charles Coughlin, had a radio show that preached his political views to millions until his rabid antisemitism and growing fondness for Nazi Germany finally became untenable. In 1938, the Federal Communications Commission—which did not yet have a formal Fairness Doctrine—stepped up pressure on radio networks to abandon Coughlin's broadcasts, and many did.

The Fairness Doctrine, adopted in 1949, dictated not only that broadcasters air controversial topics in the public interest but also that they do so in a manner that presented opposing views. But the doctrine always had enemies on the right, because, as the satirist and comedian Stephen Colbert once said, "Reality has a well-known liberal bias." By the time Ronald Reagan was elected president, those critics had accumulated enough power on the FCC to jettison the regulation. When Congress tried to codify the doctrine as law in 1987, Reagan vetoed it.

The death of the Fairness Doctrine opened a new frontier for entertaining bigots such as Rush Limbaugh, who were willing to plow over fairness, ignore fact, and spew vicious insults against liberals, people of color, women, and any other groups deemed outside the magic circle. Limbaugh, who died in February 2021, coined the term "femiNazis" for women who dared demand equality; mocked the actor Michael J. Fox, who suffers from Parkinson's disease; called global warming a hoax; and spread the racist "birtherism" claim that Barack Obama was not born in the United States. Limbaugh spawned legions of imitators, men—and a few women—who reveled in the same white grievance and vicious insults that had made the master of the form so popular.

Perhaps none of the marquee names among propagandists have done as much lasting damage to the nation's politics and culture as the lesser-known Roger Ailes, the late longtime chief executive of Fox News. A television producer, Ailes met Richard Nixon in 1967; that meeting began his stint as a media consultant to Republican politicians. Ailes believed in combative politics. The late Lee Atwater, no shrinking violet himself, once described Ailes, with whom he worked on the campaign of George H. W. Bush, as having "two speeds: attack and destroy."

In 1996, media mogul Rupert Murdoch named Ailes as head of his new venture, Fox News. Ailes imprinted the young network with his pugnacious style, his flair for sensationalism and his predilection for sexual harassment. The network brandishes the motto, "Fair and Balanced," but its content is anything but. Though Fox reporters attempt actual journalism, its popular anchors are shills for Republican politicians, conservative causes, and malignant Trumpism.

Twenty years ago, those anchors—men such as Bill O'Reilly—hewed closely to a reality-based universe, even as they denounced Democrats, mocked liberals, and pandered to the bigotry of their audience. But they were nevertheless paving the way for the presidency of Donald J. Trump, who began appearing more frequently as an on-air guest as he pondered a campaign. By the time he was elected, Trump and Fox were symbiotically bound, each needing the other, each feeding the other's worst impulses. Trump's lies were echoed by Sean Hannity, Tucker Carlson, Laura Ingraham, Maria Bartiromo, and any other on-air personality who wanted to be taken seriously in the right-wing mediascape.

The explicit racism, the brazen xenophobia, and the cartoon-ish conspiracies only grew more desperate after Trump's defeat. Fox and its downscale imitators, the One America News Network and Newsmax, have created an outlandish alternative universe of crazed and sometimes contradictory notions that compete with the most bizarre and worst-written plots of science fiction. They go so far as to encourage the weird theories associated with Q-Anon, a web of far-fetched conspiracies that center around the central claim that powerful Democrats are engaged in a global pedophilia scheme.

Fox News personalities have sown doubts about the safety and efficacy of the COVID-19 vaccine—even as Trump has complained on-air that he hasn't been sufficiently cheered for super-charging vaccine development. Some of them have suggested that the January 6 assault on the citadel of democracy was a "false flag" carried out by left-wing radicals or by the FBI. And having been inspired by ultra-conservative activist Christopher Rufo to assign all sorts of malevolence to critical race theory, they have devoted countless hours to deliberate mischaracterizations of its central thesis.

Carlson, for his part, seems engaged in a desperate campaign to make the bigots' Hall of Fame. On his show "Tucker Carlson Today," which airs on a Fox News streaming service, he conducted an admiring interview with the repugnant Charles Murray, whose widely debunked 1994 book, *The Bell Curve*, claimed that black people are genetically inferior. Carlson has also embraced the racist "replacement theory," the same view touted by the bigots who rallied in Charlottesville in 2017. In a rant in April 2021, he said:

> "I know that the left and all the little gatekeepers on Twitter become literally hysterical if you use the term 'replacement,' if you suggest that the Democratic Party is trying to replace the current electorate—the voters now casting ballots—with new people, more obedient voters from the Third World. But they become hysterical because that's what is happening, actually. Let's just say it. That's true."

That was a neatly packaged summation of the bigotry and xenophobia—the hysteria and resentment about changing demographics—that Fox is feeding to its devoted viewers. Ailes died in 2017, a year after he was ousted as a result of a sexual harassment scandal, but his vision of "fair and balanced" had already poisoned the political and cultural landscape.

Upon his death, Jeffrey Jones, director of the celebrated Peabody Awards for public service from media organizations, told the *New York Times* that "no single individual has done more harm to American democracy in the last generation. He ushered in the post-truth society."

Nevertheless, the truth is there.

Even before the current outpouring from black writers—these eloquent voices demanding a racial reckoning in the country—there were scholars like Joel Williamson, a white historian born in the South, who taught at Chapel Hill. In his 1986 book, *A Rage for Order*, Williamson wrote about the savagery of white violence and the centrality of race in the American story. He chronicled the vigilante uprisings from Wilmington through New Orleans and Atlanta, and the riots that followed outside the South. These did not stop with the Tulsa Massacre. In 1962, approximately a thousand white citizens, many of them armed, descended on the University of Mississippi to try to prevent the enrollment of a single black student. They opened fire on the U.S. Marshals assigned to protect James Meredith, while others attacked with anything that might prove lethal.

"The sickly sweet smell of tear gas filled the air," wrote journalist Karl Fleming, who covered the uprising for *Newsweek*. "The rioters seemed immune to its effects as they rushed forward hurling rocks, bottles, pieces of concrete, and steel rods—anything that could be found or torn loose."

At one point, Fleming heard the splat of two bullets in quick succession, hitting a wooden column six inches from his head. "If I were James Meredith," he muttered, "I wouldn't *go* to school with these people."

Before it was over, more than two hundred marshals and soldiers were injured. Twenty-nine were shot. Two people died. In many ways, it was a grim foreshadowing of January 6, 2021. But as Williamson makes clear in his book, the white appetite for blood went deeper, especially in the South where it often became more personal and sadistic, with consequences that were equally contagious. He wrote:

> In the early 1890s there emerged a pattern of lynching. There were definite seasons for the act—July being the most favored month. There were also favored places. Lynching tended to reoccur in areas where a lynching had happened before. . . . Ordinarily, there were hundreds and sometimes thousands of spectators. It was not uncommon for railroads to run special "excursion" trains to the site . . . . Lynchers knew what they were doing. Hanging with a quick breaking of the neck, hanging with strangulation, shooting, hanging and shooting, burning, slow burning, dragging, and cutting were all used to kill. . . . Rapists ordinarily suffered the loss of sexual organs. Bodies were always left in plain sight for some time after death, a deterrent for those who might be deterred. Fingers, toes, ears, teeth, and bones were common souvenirs. A pro-lynching governor of South Carolina, Cole Blease, received the finger of a lynched black in the mail and planted it in the gubernatorial garden.

Between 1901 and 2018, the U.S. Congress tried and

failed more than two hundred times to pass a bill to outlaw the practice. During the Roosevelt Administration, after First Lady Eleanor Roosevelt joined the NAACP, she lobbied her husband to support the fight for anti-lynching legislation. FDR refused. He did not want to alienate the South. Statistics are sketchy and incomplete, as the number of these ritual executions soared into the thousands. During the 1890s, they occurred at the rate of at least two a week, and though the majority were in the South, not all were. And there is also this. On the wall of the Equal Justice Initiative's Legacy Museum in Montgomery, where the goal is to reveal a tapestry of connection between the present and the past, signage notes that in 2015, unarmed black citizens were killed by police at the rate of two a week—a number that mirrored the pace of lynching at its peak.

Is this simply a coincidence of history? Perhaps it is. But after the murder of George Floyd, many Americans were confronted by the fact that at the very least his death was not an aberration. The question we all had to answer—and one that remains unanswered—was what exactly we would do about it.

In the anguish that followed Floyd's death, a Southern-born black scholar at an Ivy League school turned to the writings of James Baldwin, searching for answers to his own disillusionment. Eddie S. Glaude, Distinguished University Professor of African American Studies at Princeton, came of age, he says, as "a country boy from Moss Point, Mississippi." He understood the cruelties of the place he was born, but he also knew that in an earlier generation, Baldwin had found a measure of hope in the South. That was where he found the civil rights movement— that improbable, inevitable moment of reckoning when Martin

Luther King and a cast of thousands sought to "compel a national confrontation with the truth." But King was murdered and the nation turned away, and Baldwin was left to wrestle with despair.

In *Begin Again: James Baldwin's America and Its Urgent Lessons for Our Own*, Glaude wrote about a visit to the south of France—a pilgrimage after Trump became president to the ruins of a house where Baldwin had lived as an expatriate.

> The ruins were a fitting description for what Baldwin saw in the latter part of his life in the United States. He saw decay and wreckage alongside greed and selfishness. He saw, and felt deeply, the effects of America's betrayal of the black freedom struggle of the mid-twentieth century: The country had refused, once again, to turn its back on racism and to reach for its better angels, and our children were paying the cost. As I looked out onto the ruins and thought of the election of Donald Trump and the ugliness that consumed my country, I asked myself: What do you do when you have lost faith in the place you call home? That wasn't quite the right way to put it: I never really had faith in the United States in the strongest sense of the word. I hoped that one day white people here would finally leave behind the belief that they mattered more. But what do you do when this glimmer of hope fades, and you are left with the belief that white people will never change—that the country, no matter what we do, will remain basically the same.

Glaude knew America had been here before, more than once, in fact. It was not hard to imagine, if you could bear it, the disillusionment at the end of Reconstruction when equality in the eyes of the law—that civic affirmation of fundamental humanity—was snatched from those so recently enslaved. How did they hold onto hope, at least enough so they could survive? And how do we do it in our own time—this third opportunity for a national redemption after the betrayals of Reconstruction and the civil rights movement?

After the murders of the 1960s—Dr. King, Medgar Evers, Malcolm X—Glaude writes that Baldwin, though consumed with despair, "held on to his faith in the possibility of a moment when we could all be fully ourselves." Perhaps, he thought, our current generation could find the same faith—on the other side of our own despair:

> Donald Trump's presidency unleashed forces howling beneath our politics since the tumult of the 1960s. For decades, politicians stoked and exploited white resentment. Corporations consolidated their hold on government and cut American workers off at the knees. Ideas of the public good were reduced to an unrelenting pursuit of self-interest. Communities fractured. Demographics shifted. Resentments deepened. The national fabric frayed, and we are all at one another's throats. The restless ghosts underneath our politics now haunt openly . . . A moral reckoning is upon us, and we have to decide, once and for all, whether or not we will truly be a multiracial democracy.

The writers of this book, one black, one white, both of us Southern, share that sense of moral urgency. We have seen redemption in our own haunted place, and we understood what John Lewis meant when he said he found more hope in the

South than in any other part of America. We saw some of that hope in 2020, and there have been reminders for the past fifty years. We have hoped that others would see them too—would find in the lives of John Lewis or Dr. King, of Stacey Abrams or Jimmy Carter, of Raphael Warnock and Jon Ossoff, an antidote to our darker exports—our Southern legacy of bitterness and fear, of violence, rooted so deeply in the issue of race.

The arc of the moral universe is long, but it bends toward justice. This was Dr. King's affirmation at the end of the Selma to Montgomery March.

We are still not sure if we should believe him.

In her best-seller, *Caste*, Isabel Wilkerson remembers a question of dread posed by civil rights historian Taylor Branch during a particularly dark time in the Trump presidency. Branch, a white Southerner whose fascination with civil rights led him to write the prize-winning trilogy, *America in the King Years*, had been musing with Wilkerson about the country's long history of inequality. In Wilkerson's view, this mix of white supremacy and caste, often reinforced by violence, remained a threat to our founding ideals and seemed to be reaching critical mass. "So the real question would be," Branch replied, "if people were given the choice between democracy and whiteness, how many would choose whiteness?"

America has made that choice before—at the end of Reconstruction, certainly, and maybe at other times as well. Now it hangs in the balance again.

It may not be long before the answer is clear.

- 30 -

Index